D1383105

# 42 Rules for Outsourcing Your Call Center (2ⁿᵈ Edition)

Best Practices for Outsourcing Call Center Planning, Operations and Management

## By Geoffrey A. Best

E-mail: info@superstarpress.com
20660 Stevens Creek Blvd., Suite 210
Cupertino, CA 95014

Published by Super Star Press™, a Happy About® imprint
20660 Stevens Creek Blvd., Suite 210, Cupertino, CA 95014
http://42rules.com


2$^{nd}$ Edition: November 2012
1$^{st}$ Edition: September 2011
Paperback ISBN (2$^{nd}$ Edition): 978-1-60773-109-2 (1-60773-109-6)
Paperback ISBN (1$^{st}$ Edition): 978-1-60773-068-2 (1-60773-068-5)
eBook ISBN: 978-1-60773-069-9 (1-60773-069-3)
Place of Publication: Silicon Valley, California, USA
Library of Congress Number: 2011936233

## Trademarks

## Warning and Disclaimer

# Praise For This Book!

*"Geoffrey has written the comprehensive resource for understanding the complexities of modern day contact center management. From customer experience design to the fundamentals of IT infrastructure, this book provides the not only the right topics, but also the deeper insights required to maximize the effectiveness of a contact center operation. I highly recommend this book whether you're an experienced contact center leader or someone that needs to quickly learn the intricacies of outsourcing."*
**Scott McIntyre, Chief Instigator, Infinite Green Consulting**

*"42 Rules is a real-world, practical guide that helps anyone from the newly indoctrinated contact center manager to the seasoned veteran navigate the difficult terrain in outsourcing their call center operations. I've worked side-by-side with Geoffrey during a recent outsourcing engagement and he follows his own advice to deliver success and ensure that both parties achieve an optimized outcome. This book is a must read for all contact center professionals."*
**Ron Becht, Director Ecommerce Operations, Advance Auto Parts**

*"Geoffrey has captured the fundamentals for how to outsource a call center in a logical step-by-step process that exposes the reader to real-life scenarios. 42 Rules for Outsourcing Your Call Center provides an encompassing view into what is necessary to plan and deploy a call center using a BPO and I recommend it for anyone that is contemplating this challenging task."*
**Nick Jiwa, Managing Director of CustomerServ, LTD**

*"42 Rules for Outsourcing Your Call Center is a tremendous guide for both the novice and the experienced managers working with the complexities of call center outsourcing. I worked with Geoffrey putting together a call center from the ground up. Geoffrey writes from hard experience and has shared his knowledge for those who want to avoid the problems we shared first hand."*
**Ray Smithers, CEO, Akos Technologies, LLC**

*"Geoffrey Best has written an outstanding guide to outsourcing call centers. Based on his many years of experience, he has masterfully considered all aspects and challenges of this process. You won't find this kind of practical advice anywhere else. This book is a must read for any company considering or implementing outsourcing."*

**Rosemary Coates, President of Blue Silk Consulting, author of *42 Rules for Sourcing and Manufacturing in China***

"Knowledge is sometimes more useful to others than to those who possess it. What we know is a drop, what we ignore is an ocean."
- Issac Newton

## Dedication

To my friends and colleagues who have guided me in my career; to my wife, Nurcan, and my sons, Graham and Aaron, who have been patient with me during life's journey, and to my daughter-in-laws, Irene and Jessica, who have given me my grandchildren Caleb, Casey, Charlotte, and Garrett with the reaffirmation that the journey will continue.

# Contents

Contents

# Introduction

*42 Rules for Outsourcing Your Call Center* is a compilation of real-life problems, lessons learned, pitfalls found, and practical approaches I have experienced during my career. Rather than providing just a tutorial on best practices, I looked at ways to share the knowledge of the many talented people I have known in my career in a manner that is easy to digest by novices and experts alike. While novices may see the book as an introduction to call center outsourcing, I hope that experts will enjoy the book and recognize their own experiences that are similar to mine.

I use the term "call center" as a generic term for any organization that is serving customers. The functions of the traditional call center are expanding. Agents that once only worked with the telephone now use instant messaging, Short Message System (SMS), social media engines, and email. Some people in the industry are beginning to refer to call centers as contact centers where agents use these multiple media forms to communicate with the public. My rules are common to all organizations that interact with their customers. Thus, I use the traditional term, call center, unless specifically referring to those capabilities that require contact center functionality.

## Why 42 rules?

In *The Hitchhiker's Guide to The Galaxy*, the number 42 is referred to as revealing the answer to life, the universe, and everything. I cannot attest to navigating the universe, but I am sure if you are reading this book it is because you are looking for a simple and concise way to understand what is involved in the complex task of outsourcing. Perhaps you have already been involved in outsourcing a call center. If you have, then navigating the universe may seem simple in comparison. After all, when navigating the universe, you do not have to convince management of your ideas, deal with changing requirements, or manage a multitude of tasks that need to converge on a single date to go live.

Having a galaxy of options may seem advantageous when first looking at entering the stream of sequential decisions necessary for outsourcing your call center. The reality is that too many options sometimes may result in choosing the wrong path. Once chosen, that path may lead to unexpected directions with unseen "pitfalls" that may ultimately affect your business's reputation for customer care.

Industry success with customer service is becoming more and more difficult to attain. Everyone has a story about poor customer service and more often than not, the story involves a call center. In austere times, customer service becomes even more important as companies learn the hard way that answering the phone is not enough.

*In Search of Excellence* by Thomas J. Peters and Robert H. Waterman Jr. was written in 1982 when times were hard for America. The national unemployment rate was above 10 percent, inflation was running at about 14 percent per annum, and the Federal Reserve Board had increased interest rates. The country was in recession.[2] Yet, this book tells of companies that did well during this economic downturn because they focused on customer satisfaction being better than their competitors. Economic times are not always hard, but providing excellent customer service always pays for itself in increased sales and customer loyalty.

How to outsource your call center and still achieve excellence in customer care is what I have tried to capture in these rules. *42 Rules for Outsourcing Your Call Center* places a heavy emphasis on planning every aspect of your project, obtaining technical and executive commitments, validating and re-validating your assumptions, and executing your deployment with a methodology. Each rule offers you recommendations (that can limit risk and help avoid failure) and a road map that deals with the large number of options you will confront when outsourcing a call center.

# 1

# Rules Are Meant to Be Broken

**Experience defines when and how rules can be broken if you understand why the rule is as it is and are absolutely sure it will work when broken.**

The theory that any number of rules, even 42, can quantify how businesses define the essence of call center outsourcing is idealistic. Rules cannot provide an exact business strategy. Moreover, strict adherence to rules denotes that decisions are black and white, setting forth a narrow path for organizations to follow. Businesses, including call centers, are inherently dynamic, sometimes requiring rapid changes in strategy and operations to achieve their objectives.

In contrast to the black and white nature of rules, guidelines introduce shades of gray and enable general directions, rather than narrow paths. Guidelines can be established with the knowledge that there is enough flexibility along the path to allow pitfalls to be avoided before they appear.

The flexibility of a guideline recognizes that every business is unique. Their goals, methods, and products are all different, even in the same industry. So the probability is small that rules for one company will work the same way, if at all, in another. But experience in both companies is essential to understand the differences.

### Experience Provides Knowledge

Experience provides the knowledge of not only *when* to follow rules, but also *if* the rules should be followed. Rules can be broken if you understand why the rule is as it is and are absolutely sure it will work when broken.

Experience also provides insight for when to accept rules you don't understand and are best not broken.

This introduces a dichotomy for following the 42 rules. Innovation cannot happen without breaking rules. Consider the quotation from Steve Jobs that "It's better to be a pirate than to join the navy."[3] Steve Jobs seemingly broke the technology rules of the day, and consequently became an industry leader because he followed the rules for successful marketing.

Breaking rules to achieve innovation is always a temptation amongst imaginative people. Creative rule breaking is what separates the good from the great, the ordinary from the inspiring. It may also turn well-planned strategies into failures, and may distinguish the difference between being creative and being a novice. Even experts can make mistakes when trying a new technology or a new technique. You may have been in a meeting where everyone applauded the use of a new technology only to discover there were a number of issues discovered during implementation.

## Be Careful of Novices

Often, novices don't know that a rule exists. Even when they do, they don't think it applies, or they don't understand why the rule is there. Novices may ignore proven techniques only to discover they have missed an essential step when the pressure is on to meet deadlines, increase productivity, or deal with component failures.

We were all novices once and experience comes from learning. If you are breaking a rule to better understand why it is what it is, then it is part of an educational process. However, if time and money are involved, following rules has its benefits. After all, it is much better to have a success on your resume than a lesson learned.

So while 42 Rules cannot guarantee success, they can identify areas where the potential for the loss of time and money may be avoided. And, isn't that why experience rules?

# 2

# Ask "Why Outsource?"

**Understanding industry trends versus internal workloads, costs, and schedules.**

Asking the question "Why Outsource?" would seem to be counter to general economic movements and run against prevailing industry beliefs. Many companies are outsourcing as standard procedure, following industry trends. Yet, the question needs to be asked. After all, call centers have been supporting the needs of customers since the telephone was offered to the public, and cost has always been a factor in the history of call centers.

Even from the beginning, Alexander Graham Bell at the Boston Telephone Dispatch company hired the first female telephone operator, Emma Nutt, on September 1, 1878 for two reasons: lower costs and higher customer satisfaction.[4]

Bell determined that women were better behaved than young men. Women had pleasant voices that customers—most of whom were men—preferred. They could also be paid less and supervised more strictly than their male counterparts.[5] Since then, women have obtained equal treatment and equal pay, but the ability to calmly handle customers with courtesy and patience has set standards that have lasted for more than 100 years.

Businesses are still challenged to find ways of minimizing costs and maximizing profits while retaining their customer through service excellence. So when making the decision to outsource, businesses are seeking outsourcers with abilities to deliver high customer satisfaction plus cross-sell/up-sell revenue instead of being just a low-cost provider.

Many businesses also realize they are not that good at running their own call centers and are looking for an outsourcer with core capabilities in call center operations and customer service. The top outsourcers have tens of thousands of agents in call centers around the world with the best technology available and the ability to leverage their scale and efficiency in ways your company cannot duplicate.[6]

Still, you need to know how to project the load for inbound and outbound calls, the life cycle of the product or services, and the level of service to be maintained. This may vary between outsourcing inbound services and outbound services. For outbound call centers, planning the workload is relatively easy. The number of agents will be dependent on the number of calls to be dialed.

In contrast, the rate that inbound calls will be received is harder to predict. You may not get any calls for minutes, and then receive a rush of calls at one time. Thus, forecasting your call patterns is critical to determining whether to outsource or not. If the staffing model is too high, the cost benefits are minimized. If the staffing model is too low, customer service will suffer.

Businesses operating internal call centers should have historical reports with how many calls are received in late August versus those received during the holidays between Thanksgiving and Christmas. The same reports should tell you how many calls are received Monday versus Thursday, or even for specific times of the day. Analyzing the data should reveal patterns that can be used for forecasting, as long as factors that could alter the patterns are taken into consideration.

Your forecasting may improve over time, but it is impossible to accurately predict how many calls you will receive at specific times, days, or seasons. The only fact you can count on is that call flow will not be even. From time to time, agents will be idle. At other times, callers will be waiting for the next available agent.

So why ask if you should outsource? The answer depends on establishing the expectations of how an outsourcer will handle your calls. There are many variations on outsourcing with no off-the-shelf solutions. Each solution depends on your business expectations, goals, and objectives. Moreover, you need to be sure your unique needs will be met and your outsourcer is capable of meeting your expectations for cost and customer service.

# 3 Define an Outsourcing Approach

Developing an outsourcing approach is easier when segmented into phases. For example, phases may include developing an outsourcing strategy, understanding technology options, identifying your risks, evaluating and selecting an outsourcer, preparing for your first go live call, and providing ongoing management.

If you have already answered the first question of, "Why Outsource?" in the initial phase, then you will need to go further and ask, "What type of outsourcer do I need?" "How will this change my business processes and organization?" and "What are the risks?"[7]

Without asking these questions and jumping directly to the process of vendor selection, you potentially expose your company to one of the biggest factors in a failed outsourcing project. That important factor is not taking the time to understand the requirements, the potential impacts, or the risks.

Take the time to understand your technology options based on your requirements as your next phase. This is more than just determining what functions to outsource. It is setting operational and technical goals and objectives along with methods to achieve them. It is setting timelines for implementation and deployment. Most importantly, it is obtaining business and technology management commitment for the goals, objectives, and timelines.

Your next phase should identify your risks. This will help you understand probable issues, proactively assign resources, or take actions to minimize and control the probability or impact of each hazard.

There will be times when you need multiple outsourcers, even for the same project. In the phase to evaluate and select an outsourcer, you may determine that your project has two completely different purposes, each with distinct requirements. One project may focus on improving your overall business process with supplemental staff. Another may target business transformation to achieve cost savings or increase revenue.

Document your requirements for every project and solicit responses from potential outsourcers. Then, evaluate the responses to determine which outsourcer best fits your needs for each project. Simply putting out an a Request for Proposal (RFP) and taking the lowest bidder may work in some cases, but companies need to remember that successful outsourcing projects ensure your customers have an excellent experience.

Part of your evaluation should ensure your outsourcer complies with any federal or local legislation your company is obligated to follow. Companies make considerable investments to ensure they are compliant with legislation to protect customers' personal and financial information. Your evaluation needs to make sure any potential outsourcer can guarantee the continuation of the compliance you have obtained.

The subsequent phase selects the outsourcer and begins the preparation for your first go live call. This includes planning for your outsourcer's readiness of facilities technology, security, and agent training. This phase should deal with organizational and procedural changes in your company. You may have executive support for the processes being outsourced, but there may be some members of your company who will fight those changes. It may take a long time to fully implement the changes that outsourcing brings with it. However, if the outsourcing contract is terminated, it also takes time to bring it back in-house.

Going-live is an exciting time and may include formal openings and witnessing an agent reply to the first customer. Each go live event is unique and should be advertised as a successful accomplishment for all involved.

Even after the go live phase, you need ongoing management and monitoring of your outsourcer operation. One of the best ways to maintain communication with your outsourcer is through a Command Center, both, theirs and yours. Command Centers become the hub for managing daily operations and escalating issues when things go wrong.

The last phase ensures the quality of the customer experience is maintained. This phase will be the most difficult and should not be left to the outsourcer. More than likely, you should expect to increase your internal costs for quality control and plan to work extensively with your outsourcer over the period of the contract.

# 4 Know Your Customer Expectations

**Knowing what your customer expectations are is easy. They are high.**

Knowing your customer expectations is easy. They are high and they expect you to meet them. Your customers are calling your call center because they need help to purchase a product, resolve an account issue, maintain a product, or ask any number of questions that they believe your call center can assist them with. It may seem odd that your customer's expectations are high because many callers may be anxious, frustrated, or even short-tempered. However, if their expectations were not high, then they would probably not be a customer of your business or products. They would be someone else's.

This is a very advantageous position, but one that needs to be considered when outsourcing your call center. Even if the customer has received an error in billing or the product/service is deficient, customers will still have a high expectation that when they call, the issue will be remedied. If their expectations are not high, the odds are that this is because the customer has not been able to obtain the assistance they expected, and you are in jeopardy of losing them.

One would think that if customer expectations are high to begin with, it should be easy to provide the caller with an experience that maintains them as a good customer. Conversely, the disadvantage to this assumption is that any call center can only *meet* the expectation of their customers. Agents can rarely exceed them. Worse yet, there is a high potential that call center agents may fail unless proper planning and training are in place.

The primary objective of meeting customer expectations is **First Call Resolution (FCR)**. FCR means exactly what is says, and it is what customers expect. Customers call with the expectation that whatever problem they may have, the agent will be able to remedy it in a single call.

To help meet these expectations, agents should have:
- Access to systems with a single view of the customer data
- Training in how to engage the customer, build a relationship, and meet the customer needs
- Authority to solve the customer issues, including setting aside the rules to meet customer expectations
- An awards program that encourages First Call Resolution

Agents who are not able to service the caller during their first interaction may mean customer dissatisfaction. Moreover, if the customer requires multiple contacts, your company is at a higher risk of losing the customer relationship.

A second objective of meeting customer expectations is for the agent to build a relationship with the customer. This unique interchange between customer and agent occurs almost instantaneously with the initial salutation. It continues for the next six to ten minutes, or longer, to maintain that relationship. In that small amount of time, the agent has to gain the customer's trust, overcome any previous issues, and remedy the current problem.

To establish this relationship, agents need to present themselves as people the caller can immediately identify with. This may start with a simple greeting that sets the tone for the rest of the call. It may be an introduction from the agent having immediate access from a customer database that lets the caller know the agent understands the relationship between the caller and your company. For example, if a customer calls a bank and the agent knows the type of accounts the caller maintains, an immediate relationship is formed based on the customer feeling he is valued—which is what the customer expects.

More often than not in this era of outsourcing, this relationship is not established. What is more, there are few ways to know that the relationship has not met customer expectations.

I am sure you have experienced a customer service call in which an agent asked if you were satisfied with the services you received. If you were, you agree. Like most callers, if you were not satisfied, you say simply yes just to end the call. This may be a false signal to the company that their agents are meeting customer expectation, when in fact their agents have faltered. Moreover, your opinion of the company as one providing quality customer services may have changed without the company knowing why.

# Communication Is the Key to Customer Relationship

**Outsourcing initiatives often fail because the implementation is not focused on building a relationship with their customers.**

Managing customer relationships commonly refers to the process used by companies to track and organize one or more contacts with its customers. To assist in this process, many companies use software referred to as **Customer Relation Management (CRM)**. CRM solutions can manage many aspects of customer contact from front office customer service to back-office operations such as billing and order fulfillment. The industry is filled with CRM vendors, but CRM needs to be more than just implementing a software solution. It needs to be a holistic program that deals with all facets of customer contact.

Perhaps the most important characteristic of your relationship with customers is for your agents to communicate in a manner that immediately establishes trust with them.

In his book, *Blink*, Malcolm Gladwell describes adaptive unconscious as the ability to formulate an opinion of someone in the blink of an eye. Consider that in the instant an agent greets a customer, the customer may have already formulated an opinion as to whether the agent will or will not be able to help them.

Thus, when an agent greets a customer with a name that is clearly not his own, but taken to create familiarity with the American culture, it may do the exact opposite and create an unexpected distance. After all, if an agent introduces himself with a name that is not his, your adaptive unconscious may ask what else is not true.

Americans like dealing with the truth, even if they cannot pronounce the name.

The other issue with communications is that Americans tend to use jargon and colloquialisms. It is not a good trait, but it is a real trait. When agents talk to customers, they must be adept with common colloquialisms and understand the use of inflection when speaking. Consider the word "right." It can be used to mean right as opposed to left or correct as opposed to incorrect. However, if spoken with the proper inflection, it can be treated as sarcasm and meant to comment that something is "not right."

This is just one example, but certainly not the only word in the English language that can be used in multiple ways. English can be a simple language. Understanding how the language is used can be complex, a fact you must be cognizant of when outsourcing your call center offshore.

Call centers establish relationships with conversation, manners of speech, and common dialect. Agents need to be professional—yet familiar—with the caller and able to distinguish the context of words with multiple meanings.

If the agent and the customer cannot communicate easily, the burden of the relationship is placed on the customer. The customer may have to use simple words to be understood, speak slowly, or repeat their request several times. This role reversal can lead to high customer dissatisfaction and a tarnished reputation.

Consider the lessons of Dell India; a subsidiary of the US based Dell Inc.[8] In 2001, Dell outsourced technical support to Bangalore, India. By late 2003, Dell had received so many customer complaints about the difficulty of communicating with their agents, it stopped sending US technical support calls for two of its corporate computer lines to the Bangalore center and redirected the calls to US facilities.

Dell has since committed major resources to improving their support image with agents that are better trained in English and American culture and no doubt, will continue to make improvements.

However, there are questions that are still asked. Was the decision to outsource a profitable one? Did Dell's issue of effective agent communication enable HP to capture additional market share? No doubt there are any number of different answers, but the important point is that the question of technical support agents being able to effectively communicate with their customers didn't exist prior to Dell's outsourcing.

# 6 Determine Communication Modes

**Offer your customers Voice, Chat, email, or Mobile Phone SMS to request service.**

When you first thought of outsourcing your call center, you most likely pictured rows of agents on the telephone at a vendor site. However, customers in today's society, especially younger customers, use a variety of ways to communicate, including instant messaging and social media. Even email for this new generation is passé.

If your company is already using these methods, then you are ahead of, or in line with your competitors. If you are still using just voice, consider the use of these voice alternatives for increasing customer loyalty and gaining a competitive edge. Your choice is to determine which modes of communications to support and how to manage them in an outsourced environment.

At a minimum, your company is probably supporting customers with email and already understands the lower cost of email support over voice calls. Then again, email is not ideal for interactive two-way dialogue and is prone to miscommunication.

Texting with your customers is interactive and helps to ensure the dialog will end in satisfactory resolution of the service request on the first attempt. Obviously, texting has its own issues with heavy usage of abbreviations such as "BRB," "TY," and "RUT" respectively meaning, "be right back," "thank you," and "are you there."

Communication through texting allows your customers to initiate a dialogue from their existing IM client or through your website. It also allows your call center to contact a customer on their IM client when the customer is available for a callback no matter how a service request was received. Lastly, if an agent is having difficulties responding to requests, he can bring in other experts into the text session, either privately or in a three-party session with the customer.

Outsourcing the ability for your customers to text an agent requires the same planning and preparation as voice communications with some differences. When a customer requests service through messaging, there still needs to be a response to let them know who they have reached. If an agent is not available, your system needs to provide an automated reply to the IM customer to let them know they are in a queue. Such a message can provide the same information as music on hold, including how much time the IM customer will have to wait in queue or alternatives to waiting.

In voice communications, inbound calls may be routed to agents with the most appropriate skills to handle the call. The same requirement applies to inbound messaging. Customers requesting service using text messaging need to be intelligently routed to the most available agent who can best handle the media and the issue. If the customer has waited for more time than your limit or the queue length threshold has been exceeded, the IM request can be escalated to a supervisor or a higher tier of agent.

Inbound calls may also use a caller ID to extract a customer record from a database and then use an adjunct system to "pop" the customer record on an agent screen when the call is routed to the agent phone. Texting can provide a similar functionality using one of the several commercial packages available. As customers send a message, these systems can identify them by their instant message identifier if the customer has registered their "handle" with you in a previous session. The solution can then access a related customer record, attach the data to the interaction, and assist the IM agent with the customer profile.

If planned properly, extending the modes of communications can enhance your customer service image and enable your company to increase its service levels. After all, agents on the phone can only handle one call at a time. Agents responding to messaging can handle multiple chat sessions or SMS messages at the same time. This may substantially change your staffing model and can appreciably reduce your customer service costs.

# 7 Govern Work-at-Home Agents

**How do you manage agents not in the office.**

A recent trend for keeping costs down while using domestic agents is enabling outsourced agents to work at home. This is not a new concept. In the early days of telephone service, many rural telephone operators worked at home with a switchboard provided by the telephone company. Almost a century later, the cycle of centralization and decentralization provided an opportunity for women to again work at home. This cycle started in 1956 when Phonepower started the first answering service with eight operators in Altoona, PA. By the 1970s, telephone company's electronic switching systems enabled operators to pick up calls dialed to another number and appear to be in the same business around the clock.

Companies are again looking at the benefits of agents working at home as an alternative to sending calls off shore. This renewed approach can offer competitive pricing with domestic agents where a strong understanding of the American culture is necessary. The opportunity to work at home attracts stay-at-home moms and dads, teachers, business people, and professionals. This workforce can provide skilled, high quality, and loyal employees who enjoy talking to people, logging orders, processing transactions, providing customer assistance, or making various types of reservations with a minimum of supervision. It is also a cost-effective method for addressing business continuity and disaster recovery. In the event of a pandemic outbreak, such as a serious flu, agents who normally work in a call center can work at home without the fear of contacting or spreading disease.

Still, you will need to hire, manage, monitor, and reward these remote agents as you would premise-based agents. This may add costs that offset your savings, but should not deter you from evaluating home agents. Consider that some of the best processes for managing a remote workforce have been used to manage agents in secondary locations.

The benefits of moving your agents, or your outsourcer's workforce, from a brick and mortar environment to a situation where the agent pays for the overhead are obvious. Although there are still companies that supply at-home employees with the equipment necessary to work remotely, most companies are looking for the home agents to supply their own computers, Internet access, and telephone service.

Keep in mind the environment of the home is much different from thirty or forty years ago, as is the domestic culture of society. High speed Internet may be widely available, but security is a predominant factor in our daily lives.

Consequently, while the economics of work-at-home agents are attractive, security safeguards must be employed to ensure the confidentiality of your customer data. While this may appear achievable through strict procedures for the home agent, it is better accomplished through technical means.

The industry offers many solutions for secure connections, but you should select one that can also verify a number of preconditions before a home agent can connect to your network. For example, the solution technology may query the home agent's personal computer network and device settings, including scanning for malware. The pre-check can verify the operation of endpoint security software such as antivirus applications. Moreover, the technology should be used to grant or deny access based on your corporate security policies.

The technology should also only allow access to your applications through a secure means where agents work in what is known as a protected workspace. A protected workspace means that if your application writes data to the local disk drive in the agent's personal computer, the protected workspace encrypts the data while the agent is logged in and destroys the data when the agent logs out. This helps to ensure that your data will not be copied, printed, saved, or sent through email or web chats. Just because your agents are not on premise does not mean your outsourcer can forego managing them as if they were.

# 8 Integrate Social Networking

**Social networking is the new word of mouth.**

Word of mouth has always been an effective tool for branding your company's reputation for customer service. It is so powerful that there is even a Word of Mouth Marketing Association, WOMMA (http://womma.org) that offers training, standards, and best practices to its members. WOMMA defines word of mouth as "The act of consumers providing information to other consumers."[9]

The Internet extends that word of mouth power to a completely new level through online social media networking. The experiences of an individual were once limited to influencing a small group of people, but with social media, these experiences can now have a huge impact that touches customers on a worldwide basis. Consider that Facebook topped 200 million users in 2009.[10] In 2011, it had 500 million users with 50 percent active on any given day.[11] Imagine those users being able to review the customer service experience of others just by typing a few key words into a search window. More importantly, your customers can share their experiences with your company in the same audience.

If you determine that social networking should be part of your customer service strategy, you will need to define how to use an outsourcer to achieve successful results. Social networks should be viewed as any other communication media with mechanisms for reporting metrics. Thus, as you consider potential outsourcers, you need to understand how social networking has been integrated into their existing operations or define how you want the outsourcer to use your technology to establish a presence.

Using social networking for customer services is not new. Most of the predominant CRM vendors offer linkage into the popular social networking engines and are promoting the use of the technology as a strategy for developing meaningful relationships with their customers. More than half of the Fortune 100 companies are using Twitter for customer service according to the study by a public relations firm Burson-Marsteller and its digital-media unit, Proof. Yet a recent Deloitte survey concludes that organizations continue to struggle to harness social media's full potential.[12] The best recommendation is that if you commit to social networking, stay with it. Entering any social network takes time and time costs money, especially in an outsourced environment.

Determine what you need to do to represent your company in a social network. First, understand that customers use social networks as a knowledge management system. They go online and ask questions about how to obtain service for an issue, gain insight into their options, or share their experiences. Unfortunately, the knowledge they access may be partial in scope, skewed to the experiences of one individual, or just plain incorrect. Your challenge is to have agents find those customers looking for an answer and direct them to the right solution. In one recent survey, 58 percent of respondents said if they had tweeted about a bad experience, they would like the company to respond to their comment.[13]

Second, understand that you cannot staff to meet the tidal wave of comments that are online. Limit the scope of your participation to one or two social networks. Determine your hours of operation and decide if it is necessary to respond to a comment in the middle of the night or whether a response the following day is acceptable. While your customers may feel their comments deserve the highest priority, your budget may not meet their expectations. Keep in mind that participation in a social network is only one of many ways to ask for customer service.

Lastly, establish reporting to help you determine what your customers are asking, the level of activity in each social network, and if your participation is worthwhile.

# 9 Evaluate Self-Help Customer Service

**The most cost effective customer service is self service.**

In an ideal situation, customers could access your website or call your **Interactive Voice Response (IVR)** to find answers to their questions. No agents would be necessary and customers could resolve their issues using self-service techniques. Unfortunately, there is no ideal situation. Customers believe their issues are unique and require special attention from a customer service representative that cannot be solved through an IVR or website.

However, even though the rate of issue resolution is low, there is still a movement to serve customers in a manner that is devoid of human interaction. Consider that the general population increasingly accepts online shopping. We even call the first Monday after Thanksgiving Cyber Monday because of the volume of online sales.

Self-help is gaining acceptance. Banks have 24/7 ATMs; gas stations have "pay at the pump," airlines have check-in kiosks; and grocery stores have self-checkout lanes. These solutions all provide quick and easy solutions to experienced customers.

What about customer loyalty? Many companies believe that customer loyalty requires human interaction. Nonetheless, are you any less loyal to your bank because you use an ATM and not a teller? This is a paradigm shift from classic thinking, but there are still some things to consider.

Self-service requires follow-up. It doesn't have to be immediate, but it does need to be there. Online stores email you a confirmation of your purchase. A few retail stores also offer the option of emailing your receipt after a purchase. A small number of companies providing home service will email you a picture of the repair person before they arrive as a measure of safety and personal security.

## Enter the Smart Phone

A new entry into self-service is the smart phone. Smart phones are Internet and multimedia enabled with functionality to text, email, browse the Internet, take pictures or video, and play multimedia. Oh, and one more function: it also operates as a mobile phone.

Smart phones have evolved since 1992 when IBM first demonstrated a concept product called Simon.[14] Today's smart phones have the ability to run software programs like a personal computer. However, different models have unique processors with diverse operating systems. Thus, applications for one phone may not work on another. This makes providing smart phone applications more complex than for personal computers.

Developing these applications for smart phones has the inherit problems of support, upgrades, and patches. However, these applications enable customers to obtain customer service almost anywhere and anytime.

Smart phone applications enable customers to find retail locations, check balances, order products, and track shipments. But, for customer service, the value is in understanding exactly what the customer is requesting before an agent begins a chat or speaks with them. This can be accomplished by having a customer log into a secure application and selecting the type of request the customer desires. Then the customer can select the type of communication they want to use and a time they want to be contacted. In many cases, the customer may be able to achieve full self-help without an agent's intervention.

This is service on the customer's terms and can create higher customer loyalty and much lower costs. It also requires a larger investment in developing and supporting a solution or application that is compatible with the many different types of smart phones.

Outsourcing a smart phone application requires higher security as data is being transmitted over a combination of cellular network and the Internet. To increase security, companies integrate personal email, pre-registered with their account, to ensure customers are being notified of access to their information.

Newer technology will most certainly solve these security requirements as smart phone applications evolve. Your responsibility will be to ensure customers can access their data securely. But in return, you may be able to achieve a higher level of self-service that yields a healthy return on your investment.

# 10 Plan a Strategy to Achieve Business Goals

**Create a strategy to identify the assumptions and establish the framework for accomplishing each goal or objective.**

Companies outsource their call centers for a variety of business reasons. These reasons may be economic, rapid growth, reorganization, or change in product direction. Whatever the reason, businesses need to understand what their goals and objectives are and how to achieve them.

How to develop goals and objectives is beyond the scope of this book and I leave it to the business strategists to tackle those topics. This chapter emphasizes the importance of understanding goals and objectives and defining a strategy to successfully outsource your call center.

As your first step, review the business goals and objectives established by your company. They should be quantitative, measurable, understandable, and congruent. Each objective should be stated in terms such as growth, profitability, market share, and degree of vertical integration. It should also be associated with a time-line. Objectives should provide direction, establish priorities, reduce uncertainties, minimize conflicts, and aid in both the allocation of resources and the definition of roles and responsibilities. Goals should define milestones that can be measured.

Next, determine if the goals and objectives are obtainable with the resources you have been provided. Build a team from the resources with the talents and backgrounds to help achieve success.

Finally, create an implementation strategy that defines the approach to be used for each goal and/or objective.

## Creating the Implementation Strategy

The intent of creating an implementation strategy is to identify the assumptions and establish the framework for accomplishing each goal or objective internally and externally. The strategy should identify the activities that you expect your own resources to accomplish and the ones your outsourcer will need to address.

Selecting an outsourcer may be through a request for proposal or other evaluation document that includes an outline of a detailed implementation plan to meet your business goals and objectives.

Whatever the mechanism for gathering outsourcer information, you should be able to complete an outline such as the one in Appendix A—Planning the Implementation Strategy."

Completing this outline will enable you to solidify your resource requirements, understand your timelines, and estimate your budget for internal support.

Once you complete your implementation strategy, the next challenge is to execute the plan. Execution is a process. It is not the result of a single decision or action. It is the result of a series of integrated decisions or actions over time and may require a change at all levels of your organization.

A major business hurdle is that different members of your organization are likely to have different views on how to execute the strategy. Each may be focused on his/her own specific needs. A failure to agree on a common strategy can jeopardize your strategy and severely impact your implement. To avoid this hazard, you will need to identify the differences and similarities of each view and bring consensus to all members. Consider using these four simple actions in your approach.

- **Clarify** your business goals and objectives in a simple form that is easy to understand.
- **Communicate** up and down the organization and across different functions to ensure everyone knows about the execution of the business goals and objectives.
- **Align** the various teams in your organization to make sure your strategy execution becomes a necessity that will benefit everyone.
- **Measure** your success by how much of your goals and objectives are implemented.

# Understand Implementation Timelines

**No one implements anything just before Christmas.**

The amount of time to implement any project is typically underestimated, and outsourcing a call center is no exception. Unexpected events occur in any timeline that can delay or even postpone an actual go live date. There is one basic rule all call centers abide by: no one implements anything just before Christmas. In fact, most companies impose a technology freeze during the holidays to ensure that what currently works, continues to work.

Defining a timeline sets the expectations for the rest of the project. Setting the timeline beyond the foreseeable future will make it difficult to obtain commitment from executive management. Establishing a short timeline will make it harder to obtain operational and technical commitments. Balance is achieved by ensuring you have identified all of the assumptions and activities to develop a realistic timeline.

### Scope Review

Allow time to review your scope to determine if additional requirements have crept in. Scope creep is inevitable and should be managed against the overall business goals and objectives. Whether you allow the creep to become part of your initial timeline—you decide to defer the additional requirements to another phase—is a decision you must reflect on against your timeline and your business's expectations.

## Business Process Reengineering Timeline

If you are outsourcing your complete operations, which internal business areas will be impacted? If this is a partial outsourcing for the overflow of calls or a complete outsourcing for a line of business, then what are the criteria for sending calls to the outsourcer? Each of these questions may require reengineering your business process.

This presumes you already have a good understanding of the existing process flows and can identify the decision points where an external organization can be inserted. Unfortunately, few businesses have documented their call flows, and even fewer have processes that cannot be improved.

Allocate adequate time to review your call flows and business processes with your operations team. Document where calls will be directed to your outsourcer and how calls may come back if escalated.

## Infrastructure Preparation Timeline

Understand the timeline to prepare your systems and infrastructure. This may be dependent on multiple variables and may need to be refined several times. However, it is safe to assume the tasks will take a majority of the time you have allocated.

The timeline for infrastructure preparation becomes more complex since you will need to account for two diverse system infrastructures to operate as one: your infrastructure and the infrastructure of your outsourcer.

## Data Access Timeline

The time and effort required for data access is always underestimated, especially if an existing system is already in use. Having a single data source for your internal use and your outsourcer agents is inevitably preferable. If you are considering using multiple copies of data, consider that you will need to synchronize the data at very regular intervals, and you will have the question of which data copy is more current.

Allocate enough time to either build a secure mechanism for your outsourcer to access your data or to replicate a copy of your data within their infrastructure.

I have identified the major activities that will need to be scheduled to meet your specific objectives. There may be other activities that are specific to your project and you will need to schedule the amount of time needed for each task. Tasks may be sequential or they may be performed in parallel. Either way, provide adequate time for review and approval of each assignment and include time for unexpected events.

# 12 Understand Technology Objectives

**Have you ever been told that there is nothing technology cannot solve?**

Even if you are not a technologist and believe computers, networks, and telephone systems are nothing more than "black boxes," you still need to understand the technology objectives of your company, even if only at a high level.

Technology objectives are tightly aligned with your business objectives and your success. While your IT team may promote the idea that there is technology to solve most problems, you need to be sure that the technologies of your company and your outsourcer are in place to ensure your success.

Note that topics covered in this rule are distinct disciplines and may warrant individual study to fully appreciate their depth. I provide a very high level overview so you can begin to appreciate the best practices that should be considered when evaluating your technical objectives.

Technology objectives are strategies, sometimes referred to as frameworks, which are best practices to plan, implement, deploy, and monitor your technology solution. I provide a few basic objectives that should be part of your company and prospective outsourcer's strategy to implement an outsourcing solution.

### Scalability

The technology solution should support the number of users and sites under consideration. It should also be scalable to support future growth, understanding that performance is directly attributable to the load placed on the voice and data network, as well as supporting systems.

Load can be defined as the number of agents, the number of connections to your database, the amount of voice and data traffic over your network, the number of inbound/outbound circuits, or any number of other components that are involved in your solution. Thus, as the load goes up, performance on a fixed system may go down.

Your solution, and that of your outsourcer, should be designed with adequate technology resources to handle near-term requirements, yet scalable enough to accept an additional load without replacing major system components.

## Flexibility

Business needs change and your solution, as well as your outsourcer's, should be adaptable to meet the demands of new requirements. For example, the business may change greetings depending on the time of day, day of the week, or holiday. It may change the manner calls are routed to specific agents based on time of day, day of the week, or holiday. It may also provide callers with the ability to get self-help for special events, products, or services.

Flexibility also relates to managing the technology: it should be easy to trace calls through the technology and determine the cause for errors in routing, extended hold time, or a high number of calls in queue.

## Security

The technology solution must be secure, not only in the sense that it has adequate authentication for agents accessing information about your customers, but also in the sense that your systems are well protected and do not expose security vulnerabilities.

In practice, this means your technology and access to them should be locked down with internal access controls and encryptions to limit the risk of unauthorized activity. If you expect your prospective outsourcer to maintain data at their site, you will want to be sure access to their technology is also locked down.

These are not all of the technical objectives of an outsourcing program, but it will provide direction for what the black boxes should do. Moreover, asking your technologists to explain the scalability, flexibility, and security aspects of their framework will earn points with them.

# 13 Evaluate Voice Communication Options

**How will you connect to your outsourcer?**

If your strategy is to remain the initial touch point for customers calling on the phone, then you will need a method for redirecting calls from your center to one or more of your outsourcers. Such methods have traditionally used point-to-point connectivity from your voice data center to an outsourcer center for voice and data. In today's environment, you may want to consider other communication options.

Traditional voice connections use a telephone "trunk" line to connect your call center with your outsourcer. The physical trunk carries your voice traffic through the **Public Switched Telephone Network**, commonly referred to as the PSTN.

This is standard for traditional voice calls. Then again, your customers may want to use one of their other devices such as their mobile phone, wireless hand held device, PDA, or personal computer to request customer service. Your customers may also want your service centers to conform to their schedule and not be placed in a wait queue listening to music on hold until an agent picks up the phone.

To meet the demands of this new generation, solutions using traditional voice and data circuits may not be enough. One option is to use **Session Initiation Protocol (SIP)** trunking services. SIP has been available since 2005, but acceptance and wider usage has only recently occurred.[15]

SIP blends both data and voice into a single connection and allows companies to use a data connection to replace their PSTN trucks. SIP trunking can be used to establish Voice over

Internet Protocol (VoIP), video, gaming, text, call control, and others I am sure I have left out. Recent extensions to SIP add instant messaging and presence capability, which provides a status indicator about an agent's ability and willingness to chat with a customer or vice versa.

SIP trunking can also deliver better value than traditional PSTN trunking. First, there's no limit to the number of voice sessions that can be carried over a SIP trunk (other than bandwidth), whereas a traditional PSTN trunk is limited to the number of channels available.

Second, SIP can deliver what is referenced as **Unified Communications (UC)** functions to improve an agent's ability to handle multiple forms of communications. Chat services, presence, conferencing capabilities, the ability to share applications, etc., can all be delivered over a SIP trunk, allowing companies to look at purchasing UC as a service rather than investing in premise-based hardware and software.

SIP trunks also allow organizations to extend VoIP past their physical local area network (LAN), where most of the deployments are today. This removes the need for organizations to purchase gateways, bridges or other equipment that help connect the corporate VoIP environment to the PSTN. That connectivity is done within the IP telephony service provider's network, which means your enterprise does not have to incur the cost.

To deploy a SIP trunk you need only three components: an IP-ready PBX that supports SIP, an edge device to connect to a SIP trunk provider, and a service provider that offers a SIP-trunk.

As easy as that sounds, implementing SIP and it's technologies at either your site or at your outsourcer's can be challenging, especially if you plan to integrate components from different vendors. Your best option is to work with a PBX vendor that is familiar with all aspects of SIP technology to avoid undesirable results such as poor voice quality, broken audio streams, or dropped calls.

After all, the main purpose of voice communications is to provide an excellent experience for your customers on the phone.

# 14 Understand Operational Objectives

No matter how good technology may be, it is of no value unless it works. Of course, few solutions can be 100 percent operational 100 percent of the time. Therefore, it is important to understand the operational objectives of your company. Many companies strive for 99.95 percent operational uptime. But what does that mean?

Consider that in a 24-hour by 365-day call center, there are little less than 526,000 minutes. Applying 99.95 percent would allow approximately 22 minutes of down time per month. That includes the PBX/ACD, communications circuits, database servers, application systems, user desktops, or any combination that does not allow the call center to be fully operational. If your business has a target higher than 99.95 percent, then you need a level of redundancy in your technology model.

### Redundancy and Fault Tolerance

Redundancy is the implementation of functional capabilities that would be unnecessary in a fault-free environment. In redundant systems, there are multiple identical instances of the same system. If one system fails, the solution uses one of the remaining instances. For example, a call center may use multiple IVR systems. Calls may go to any of the IVRs that operate independently, but are identical in programming. If one IVR fails, calls may go to a redundant IVR and up-time is maintained.

Obviously redundancy comes with a price, but it can enable your business to meet the high availability targets if that is a requirement for your business.

Fault-tolerant systems are characterized by not having a single point of failure and enable faults to be isolated from other components. For example, computer, network components, and voice systems may be fault-tolerant using multiple power supplies. If one power supply fails, the other power supply can take over until the faulty power supply is repaired or replaced.

The distinction between redundant systems and fault tolerant systems may seem slight, but it is important to technologists who specialize in this discipline and who can provide a much deeper discussion.

## Operational Budgets

As part of establishing your operational objectives, it is helpful to verify the amount of your budget. This is important not only for your operations, but also to deploy your prospective outsourcer's solution. At a minimum, you should budget for the following:

- Voice and data network communications, or circuits, from your data center to the prospective outsourcer sites
- Voice and data network hardware and associated software costs (including operating systems, network management software, and installation).
- Software licenses for the outsourcer to access your data from the agent desktops
- Annual support costs.
- Training costs including travel
- Professional services/Internal resources (for project management, installation and ongoing system administration and support).

## Operational Participants

A critical component of establishing your operational objectives is the early involvement by all affected parties in your organization. This will ensure the deployment of the outsourcing solution reflects all of your organizational needs and that objections are aired before the project is underway.

The following groups are typically involved in an identity management project:

- Internal Call Center Operations
- Information Technology including
  - Telecommunications Team
  - Circuit Provisioning Team
  - Data Networking Team
  - Data Base Team
  - Security Team
- Human Resources
- Project Management Office

These are, by no means, all the technical or business participants you may need. Every company is unique, but understanding the operational objectives of your company, and that of your outsourcer, is paramount to your success.

# 15 Manage the Potential Impact of Risks

**Knowing the risks that can jeopardize your project enables you to manage their potential impact.**

Identifying the risks of your project is a fluid process simply because risks are always changing. Minimizing the impact of risks is known as risk management. Risk management is the identification, assessment, and prioritization of probable risks.

Knowing the risks that can jeopardize your project enables you to proactively assign resources or take actions to minimize and control the probability or impact of each pitfall. However, during the process of outsourcing, the probability of risk may change. In fact, some risks may be eliminated while others may come into play.

Risk is the positive or negative effect of an event occurring. It is computed from the probability of that event becoming an issue and the impact it will have on the customer experience during outsourcing.

The ability to manage risk is always a primary business concern and needs to be part of any presentation for obtaining a commitment. Do not avoid the topic and assume everything will operate without incident. Issues do arise and without a well-developed plan to manage risk, even small issues can become big emergencies.

In simple terms, the level of a Risk = Probability X Impact.[16] To determine the risk level of a potential incident, you need to identify the event factors including the conditions surrounding the event, the probability of the event happening, and a value (like a percentage) of the impact if the event does happen.

By placing the event factors into a matrix with an assigned weight, you can estimate the level of overall risk by understanding the potential and conditions for:

- Avoidance
- Mitigation to reduce the impact
- Transferring the risk to your outsourcer
- Acceptance with an associated budget[17]

Your risk exposure can be calculated as the risk of a fault minus the estimated cost to avoid it. A simple calculation of cost versus savings. In turn, the risk of outsourcing may be viewed as higher, or lower, than the risk of not outsourcing your call center at all. Either way, if your executives decide to proceed with their commitment, then your exposure becomes what is known as an Assumed Risk.

It is also important to monitor when risks do materialize so that planned contingencies can be implemented. Monitoring for high or medium risks is achieved by identifying cues for each of your identified risk components.

For example, when monitoring for a high-risk failure in data communications, a temporary loss of connectivity for less than a minute is a minimum risk cue; a loss for 15 minutes is a medium risk cue; and a loss of connectivity is a high-risk cue.

As risk cues show, as escalation of the risk increases, you need to be able to determine what contingencies are appropriate. Obviously, it is better to deal with an event while it is a loss-risk issue rather than a high-risk issue. Thus, monitoring risk cues becomes an important part of risk management and enables you to handle issues with contingencies early in their event cycle.

Nevertheless, do not presume that you are ready for the risks because you have planned for contingencies. The nature of risks is that they are unpredictable.

# 16 Get Executive Commitment

**Do not expect your executives to delve into, or even understand, all of the intricacies of call center outsourcing.**

Executives who manage businesses with call centers may conceive their goals and objectives under the premise that outsourcing their call centers will save money, reduce personnel issues, and alleviate additional resources by simply contracting with the right company. However, it may be up to you to present the details for how to implement their plan and to obtain their commitment to support it.

For outbound products with short life cycles, business objectives may be realized in a short term. However, for inbound products with long life cycles, achieving their objectives may require more patience and a true executive management commitment. Keep in mind that your executives are thinking at a higher level than you may be and concerned with issues such as:

- Profit margins and reducing expenses
- Increasing the company value
- Not becoming obsolete in their industry
- Opportunities for growth
- Not having to deal with personnel issues
- Not having to defend their company in legal battles
- Becoming the best in their industry

Present your implementation strategy at their level. Define the commitment for resources and budgets necessary to achieve their business goals and objectives to make call center outsourcing a success.

A corollary to Rule 5, "Communication is the Key to Customer Relationship" is to keep your presentations short and simple. Do not expect your executives to delve into—or even understand—all the intricacies of call center outsourcing. That's why they have someone like you to detail the requirements, identify the tasks, and estimate the budget to achieve their objectives.

Reaffirm the motives behind the desire to outsource. State what is necessary to maintain a high level of customer satisfaction. Be prepared to explain the prerequisites for a successful strategy and what may differ from what was first conceived. For example, companies that have successfully outsourced collections or short-term marketing campaigns may be over-simplifying the move to outsource inbound call centers.

Presentations to senior business management can be intimidating. My own experience is that you have about thirty seconds, or less, to capture their attention. If you lose their attention at the beginning, then you may have lost them for the entire presentation. Start out with a bold statement that cannot be challenged and reaffirms their goals and objectives.

Summarize what a successful call center outsourcing can achieve.
- Relate your executive's objectives to call center functionality
- Outline the actions necessary to achieve each objective
- Provide your high level timeline when objectives will be achieved and at what cost.
- What is the expected perception for customers?
  - Positive and negative customer feedback
  - How will negative customer feedback be tracked down in the areas where we have implemented action?

In addition, your presentation should identify the pitfalls of outsourcing.
- Define potential nonconformities.
  - What are their potential costs?
  - How many are there?
  - Why and when will they go away?
- What are the indicators to show if our corrective and preventive action programs will be necessary?

Identifying both the advantages and pitfalls of the project will enable your executives to obtain a realistic overview of the project. It will also reaffirm your abilities to provide a balanced review on which to base their commitment. Remember that everyone will participate in taking credit if the project is successful. If you do not identify the pitfalls, you may stand alone if issues occur. Recognizing that potential pitfalls are part of risk management and should be quantified in terms of profitability to obtain your executive commitment.

# 17 Get Technology Management Commitment

**Technology teams never have enough resources.**

After you get your executive commitment, it is important to obtain a commitment from your technology management. In fact, your executive management may want a commitment from your technology management before they provide their final approval. Thus, you may find yourself in a "which comes first, the chicken or the egg" scenario.

Prior to obtaining their commitment, your technology management may ask, "Isn't the outsourcer going to be responsible for the technology?"

The answer is dependent on how much of your technology operation can accommodate outsourcing. No matter how much or how little you are outsourcing, your technology management needs to be involved in operating the technology of your organization and supporting the technology of your outsourcer.

### Commitment for Outbound Technologies

Outbound technologies may be standalone such as a dialer solution. In its simplest form, your technology team may not need to provide any commitment for an outsourced dialer. Your business team just needs to provide a list of people to call and a script for the outsourced agents to work with.

If the outbound solution requires agents to access your databases for account or personal information, then the solution becomes more complex. Your technology team will need to provide secure agent access. It may also mean that your technology management, or your outsourcer, will have to provide a method of communications between the outsourcer site and your data center. Either way, the communications and the access methods will need to be installed, monitored, and supported. And that means a commitment by your technology management.

## Commitment for Inbound Technologies

Inbound technologies have more components. For example, there are interactive voice response systems, intelligent call routing, customer information systems, and call recording, just to identify a few. Such technologies require additional budgets for both components and resources.

How much is outsourced may depend on business factors that are outside technology. Inbound technologies are rarely completely outsourced. Rather, it is a mixture of your internal systems and your outsourcer systems.

No matter what the mixture is, your technology management may need to commit additional infrastructure. For example, to intelligently route calls, your IVR may route calls to several outsourcers. This may require an investment in call routing technology at each outsourcer ACD to regulate call volume.

## Technology Team Commitment

Your technology team's participation to define tasks and timelines is an important facet of ensuring a solid design. Technology management needs to support this participation with the understanding that while their members contribute to the team, they may not be able to perform their normal day-to-day activities. Accordingly, they may have to backfill the positions of those who participate.

## Technology Costs

Technology management also needs to commit to implementing your design objectives. This may mean expenditures in a variety of technologies to support the addition requirements for outsourcing, including:
* Voice and data network communications
* Network management
* Software for outsourcer agent desktops
* Annual support costs

This commitment will typically be associated with a request for more resources and this brings you back to the issue of which comes first, the chicken or the egg. You may need to go back to your executive management to present your technology resource needs and confirm their willingness to fund them. Expect this to be a back-and-forth process until the needs and objectives of both business and technology management are met.

# 18 Use a Structured Methodology

**Where do I begin?**

With your technology and executive approval, you are ready to begin the process of actually planning your outsourced call center. This may be when you ask yourself "Where do I begin?"

The art of planning a technical implementation has been necessary since the first computer application was released to users. Each plan is a unique creation by one or more individuals, imprinted with the image of the planners on how the different facets will fit together. An approach to define the sequence of tasks is needed to enable management to follow the implementation process and to review periodic deliverables.

One approach is to use a structured methodology with defined milestones that provides your management with insight into the creative process and enables a "disciplined" approach to achieving your goals.

Much has been written on the methodologies used for technology implementation and the impact on the business process. Your core project team should consider using one of the many methodologies that have been published. The most important reason to use a structured methodology is that it will help you avoid the mistakes of an "undisciplined" approach and gain the benefits of structured planning that includes:

- Early business management feedback
- Minimization of misunderstood requirements
- Better resource management
- Reduction of risk
- Easier assessment of project costs

- Better integration with existing systems
- Stronger model for flexibility and expansion

## Choosing a Methodology

Choosing a structured methodology can be complicated. There are many factors that can influence your decision, including, but certainly not limited to, corporate maturity, existing processes, industry "best practices," technology involved, and assumed risk. There are also different types of methodologies; one is a classic model for relatively low-technology projects that can use a logical, linear, "waterfall" approach. This may be used for timelines that are not critical and where an assessment is necessary after each step.

More complex project integrating higher technology may use a "spiral" methodology that advocates an iterative approach. Spiral methodologies are excellent when projects can be phased over a period of time and enables improvement to be implemented during each cycle.

There are also disadvantages to using methodologies. Methodologies may be abstract with little "how-to" detail. They may advocate excessive bureaucracy or lack relevance to your business objectives. Finally, they may conflict with existing processes already in place.

## Methodology Prerequisites

Prerequisites for successfully using a structured methodology include your core project team accepting the use of a methodology. Using a structured methodology requires a strong management team that advocates the need for a disciplined approach while allowing enough flexibility in the methods to navigate obstacles in the implementation of your outsourced call center. It will also require your core project team to have core competencies in both project and technology management.

The most important prerequisite is a solid knowledge of:
- People, structure, and functions of the call center organization
- Processes and procedures to be outsourced and the benchmarks used to measure success
- Technology used to support the outsourcer
- Business strategy at the operational level

This knowledge foundation will help your team adapt the life cycle activities to meet your specific outsourcing goals and meet your objectives.

## Using a Methodology

Although each organization is unique with individual requirements, common steps are involved in developing a good plan for integration of your business process with technology. These steps makeup a methodology with a four-phase approach as described in "Appendix B—Life Cycle Methodology for Call Center Outsourcing."

# 19 Validate Requirements

**Why are we doing it this way?**

Now that you have selected a structured methodology, you are ready to validate your outsourcing project requirements. Requirements define the goals of your project. Methodology defines how to achieve them.

The first step is to evaluate your business requirements in further detail. You may believe that you already understand your project goals, but this is an initial milestone in which you want to validate them with a thorough and detailed review.

Outsourcing your call center will affect processes, technology, job roles, and culture. Significant changes to even one of these areas will require an understanding of how they will affect the other areas either directly or indirectly.

Changing multiple processes, and perhaps simultaneously, is an extraordinary task and will require both your executive and technology management to provide strong and consistent support over the life of the project. If this support wanes, then it may severely cripple your chances for success. The best way for their support not to falter is to validate your requirements and document their impact on your organization.

Remember that you have already summarized what successful call center outsourcing can achieve and the pitfalls of outsourcing when you first obtained your executive commitment. These points need to be re-emphasized and substantiated by the core project team as follows.

**Validate your business requirements** against your corporate objectives and be sure your outsourced call center is implemented with the functionality and actions necessary to achieve those objectives.

**Validate your projected timelines and internal costs** for implementing the outsourced solutions. Timelines and costs may seem diverse, but an outsourcing project is a combination of implementing technology solutions within financial constraints.

**Review expected positive and negative customer perceptions.** Your executives should re-validate the use of an outsourced call center and how negative feedback will be negated, especially if you are outsourcing offshore. Executives should also review the positive aspects such as more skilled agents, longer hours of availability, and shorter wait times to answer your customer's call.

**Reaffirm the potential for nonconformities.** Your team should validate the estimated costs for corrective action when unexpected results occur. This means confirming the ability of your outsourcer to handle high volumes during periods of unexpected outages.

Each of these points merits a thorough review and may result in a lengthy document that meticulously details your business processes in text with supporting workflows. Given the diligence of this review, you may be tempted to present a document that demonstrates how thoroughly the core project team has done their review. Don't!

Reduce the requirements to one page for your executives. Cover the critical points; focus on the future state using the outsourcer; and describe the impact of outsourcing the call center on customers and business results.

Why is this important? First, your executive and technical management have other responsibilities, some of which may have higher priorities, and you want them to read it. Second, you are going to need to reiterate how you have validated your approach again and again and the shorter and simpler it is, the more understandable and compelling the reasons will be.

# 20 Plan Outsourcer Technologies

**I thought the outsourcers were the experts.**

When you outsource, it is not enough to plan only your own implementation. To ensure you are going to get the results you expect, you also need to plan how your outsourcer will deploy their technology. This may seem strange since one of the criteria for hiring an outsourcer is that they are experts. However, even the best technology can be implemented in a manner that doesn't fulfill your desired objectives.

Planning the technology for your outsourcer is about setting up guidelines for what is needed to satisfy your requirements. Why is this important? Your outsourcer's technology should be up-to-date. More importantly, it should align with your technology objectives to ensure your company is getting the highest and most secure return on your expenditure. Moreover, your technology will need to interface with your outsourcer's technology to handle calls in a uniform manner.

Consider that your outsourcing project may require calls to be directed to agents trained with specific expertise. Directing the calls will require programming a PBX/ACD, an intelligent call management system, or an interactive voice response system.

It would be ideal if everyone used the same technology, but that is rarely the case. Therefore, the best way to fulfill your requirements is to stipulate exactly how to meet them. This means that your outsourcer will need technology that you understand, are compatible with, and can continuously monitor.

To be sure your outsourcer can meet these preconditions, you will need to define the technology requirements in a RFP. The RFP should include your expectations and set the objectives for the outsourcer to meet. It should also ask the responding outsourcers to describe or define the following:

Describe the technology you are currently using and request the technology the outsourcer will use. Their response should describe their voice and data networks including the type of PBX/ACD components, network hardware, and firewalls used in their contact and data center facilities. It should also identify any issues that might be encountered to interface the two infrastructures.

Request the number of users and sites required for the initial implementation and to scale the call center to support your future growth and requirements.

Define the system performance the outsourcer should provide based on the projected load placed on the voice and data network, as well as the supporting systems. Load can be defined as the number of agents, the number of connections to your database, the amount of voice and data traffic over your network, the number of inbound/outbound circuits, or any number of other components that are involved in your solution. Thus, as the load goes up, performance on a fixed system may go down.

Stipulate the design of the outsourcer solution have ample resources to handle near-term requirements with enough spare resources to accept additional loads without replacing components already deployed. For example, the outsourcer PBX should be able to handle a rapid increase in the number of agents for a special sale without replacing it.

Define the level of elasticity in the infrastructure so the outsourcer can quickly adjust to business demands and accommodate how calls are routed based on time of day, day of the week, or holiday schedule.

Finally, define the security standards for the outsourcer to meet or exceed those of your own company. Stipulate the level of authentication for agents accessing information about your customers and provide adequate provisions to audit their systems for security vulnerabilities.

Understanding how the outsourcer will satisfy your plan is critical to your success. Don't rely on an outsourcer meeting your objectives without providing the technology they will need to use.

# 21

# Identify Dependent Technology

**Everyone relies on someone else. Every technology is dependent on another.**

After you understand your technology objectives and define how your outsourcer technology will meet them, you will still be dependent on technology outside the boundaries of your company and that of your outsourcer. These technologies tend to be utility-centric and provide your outsourcer sites with the electric power and communications connections.

Understanding the limitations of utilities may seem to be outside the realm of selecting an outsourcer. However, it is technology your outsourcer is completely dependent on.

Consider the dependency on telecommunications. Domestic call centers tend to take a reliability factor of 99.995 percent for granted.

Outsourcers assume well-known long-distance carriers are reliable and can provide reliable end-to-end service. However, in most instances, long-distance carriers rely on a **Local Exchange Carrier (LEC)** to complete the connection for the "last mile." To their credit, domestic local exchange carriers are just as reliable as long distance carriers and work with them to provide a homogenous solution.

That is not the same for offshore operations. In other countries, well-known domestic long distance carriers still rely on small-localized telephone companies to provide the last mile of connectivity. Furthermore, these LECs may be new to the up-time requirements and demands of US-based call centers.

Hence, when issues do occur, your company, your long distance company, or your outsourcer may have to deal with extracting information from a telephone company that does not share your urgency. To make things more complicated, the local exchange carrier may not have personnel who speak English.

As a result, you and your outsourcer will need to develop a strategy for redundancy.

As part of that strategy, require your outsourcer to have two long distance carriers to their site, each with diverse paths and each using a different LEC. This sounds like an easy task, but going to geographic regions where call centers are newly emerging can mean there are just a few, or perhaps only one reliable LEC. Consequently, your outsourcer may have two distinct long distance carriers who both deliver the last mile on the same wire of a single LEC. This results in a dependency on a single point of failure, the additional cost of a second long-distance circuit, but a persisten lack of redundancy from reliance on a single LEC.

Another major dependency is electric power. Call centers in the United States use domestic electric utilities governed by public utility commissions that demand reliability. When domestic electric companies repeatedly fail, they are faced with customer complaints, public hearings, and public utility commission penalties. Even with public oversight, domestic call centers install backup power generators that, when supplied with fuel, can operate for days or weeks.

Power utilities for offshore call centers may be very different from our domestic counterparts. In many countries, power is turned off for periods of the day to minimize peak loads. Power generators are typically standard for offshore sites that are serious about supporting U.S. businesses, but fuel for extended continuous operation may not be guaranteed. The consequence is that your outsourcer may not be able to provide the same level of up time demanded of domestic call centers.

Understanding all the details of where your outsourcer is proposing to deploy your call center operations is critical to your success. Be sure to research how foreign governments are supporting offshore call center operations. Many of these governments have identified outsourced operations from the United States as a strategic revenue stream to their economy. Moreover, they offer tax incentives and financial aid to ensure call center companies in their country are equipped to meet the demands of U.S. businesses interested in employing their citizens in an outsourcing operation.

One final point: be sure your contract is with the company operating in a foreign country. Most governments require incorporation in their country to do business. As a result, a contract with a domestic outsourcer may not be with the same company. Thus, any contract should clearly define dispute procedures and where they will be adjudicated.

# 22

# Define the Deployment Process

**Part of the process is to understand what is necessary for deployment.**

Deploying an outsourced call center is a process. It doesn't matter if the call center is local, in a far corner of the continental United States, or in a remote part of the world; there are sequential steps that must be taken to be successful, and each step takes time and resources. These steps are dependent on a number of factors offered by your potential outsourcer.

### Site Preparation Tasks

If your outsourcer is recommending a site already taking calls for a different client, then the number of tasks required might be minimal, provided voice and data connectivity meet your immediate needs and the floor space layout meets your requirements.

Conversely, if the outsourcer is proposing an un-prepared site, then there are multiple tasks to be completed prior to going live. Your outsourcer will need to identify tasks, associated resources, and timelines such as those that I have recommended in "Appendix B—Life Cycle Methodology for Call Center Outsourcing: Phase 3 Design and Implementation."

When the project tasks are identified, integrate the associated tasks and timelines into your plan and track the progress on a regular basis.

### Technology Preparation Tasks

Whether the potential outsourcer call site is in a prepared state, a raw state, or somewhere in between, you will need to understand the tasks your outsourcer will require to interface to your technology infrastructure.

Second, identify the tasks to enable outsourcer agents to access your applications and customer data. If you are using remote sites, then you have already started your preparation by establishing secure communications between the remote sites and your data centers. If your remote sites meet the secure access requirements of your company, then working with an outsourcer should be similar to the remote site network.

If you do not have secure remote connections, then consider that there are multiple options for extending both voice and data communications to your potential outsourcer. Your outsourcer may extend their communications from their centers to yours. Conversely, you may extend your communications to theirs. Either way, you need to identify the tasks and allocate enough time after contract award for your engineers and your outsourcer's engineers to finalize the details of connectivity.

For voice and data communications, your outsourcer will need tasks, resources, and timelines such as those I recommend in "Appendix B—Life Cycle Methodology for Call Center Outsourcing, Phase 3 Design and Implementation."

Again, integrate the completed tasks and timeline into your plan and track the progress on a regular basis

## Tasks for Agent Training

Each task for agent training requires time, usually estimated as the period necessary to teach an agent how to handle your calls. It is also the amount of time to orient the outsourcer agents to your company history, product marketing, and typical customer profile.

For the agent to access your system, the tasks need to identify the duration necessary to obtain a login to your network, configure access to your applications, and set up each agent on a voice and screen recording system.

In summary, you will need to account for all the tasks, resources, and timelines to adequately plan for your implementation and your outsourcer's preparation. At this point in your planning, it is better to plan for more time rather than less. Everyone tends to remember a published date. Bringing a date in sooner is usually not an issue. Pushing a date out brings attention to your process with questions of what happened.

# 23 Use Your IVR Wisely

**Don't tell your customers to "Press 1 for English."**

Many companies use an **Interactive Voice Response (IVR)** system to reduce costs and facilitate the handling of inbound calls. IVRs achieve their savings by asking the caller to respond to qualifying questions that can determine what agent skills are necessary to best handle their needs. In an optimal solution, an IVR can answer all of a caller's questions in a complete self-help scenario without the aid of an agent. However, optimal solutions are rare.

When outsourcing, your company should operate the IVR, especially if more than one outsourcer is used or being considered. This will give you control of the call as it is first answered and direct the caller to an agent with the appropriate skills to help them. It also means that you will need to carefully script the IVR.

IVRs are also the first point of contact between your caller and your company. Thus, how an IVR presents your company to your caller is as important as how agents answer the call. Thus, the opening verbiage of your IVR will set the tone for the rest of the call. Unfortunately, many companies begin the relationship with their customer with "Press 1 for English."

This may be politically correct and address the bilingual nature of our American culture, but it may also have a negative effect on some callers. Many Americans are sensitive to immigration issues and asking them to select English as the language they wish to converse in may prompt them to feel alienated towards your company.

Consider an alternative phase, *"Oprima el uno para continuar en Español"* (press 1 to continue in Spanish). This phase assumes you do not have to press anything to continue in English, but includes Spanish as part of your introduction.

Obviously, there are many domestic companies that focus on specific cultural markets and the reality is that every domestic call center must serve customers in a minimum of English and Spanish. However, when developing a script for the United States, assume that callers speak English. After your introduction, offer the caller the option of using a different idiom in the other languages you are supporting.

## Limit the Menu Options

Design your script with simplicity. Many IVRs offer too many menu options and the average ear has a poor memory. If you are using more than four options, the caller will opt-out for to speak to an agent. Usually, this means the caller will hit "0," even if it is not programmed in your script.

The most productive IVRs are ones with a low "opt-out" rate. This means callers select an IVR menu option without hitting a "0" to opt-out of the script. Success comes from simplicity and a single level to qualify the type of call. If you do provide scripts under primary options, do not use a script with more than three levels. Again, callers will not remember the options offered and navigating multiple levels may become too complex for the caller. Once more, callers will hit "0" for an agent if they become frustrated or impatient. If multiple levels are used, track the options and transfer the call to the most appropriate skill based on selections made by the caller.

## Natural Language IVRs

The use of natural language in IVRs is increasing with the intent of making the IVR more conversational. Natural language IVRs allow callers to speak phases or respond to questions with voice in lieu of selecting a number on the telephone dial pad. The purpose is to make the IVR more user friendly, but without careful programming, the success rate of users navigating to an ultimate selection will be low.

Finally, do not ask the caller to enter a number, such as an account or telephone number, if the number is not going to be provided to the agent who ultimately answers the call. Nothing is more irritating to a caller than telling an agent a number they just entered through their telephone keypad.

# 24 Route the Call with Intelligence

**Provide the ability to route calls to an optimum answering resource anywhere in the enterprise at any given moment.**

Routing a customer call to the most available and qualified agent is a critical objective for call centers. Call centers spend time, energy, and money to achieve a customer experience that provides prompt service with an agent who can resolve the caller's issue.

In its simplest form, calls can be routed by dialing different **Toll Free Numbers (TFN)**, each associated with a **Dialed Number Identification Service (DNIS)**. DNIS is a service sold by telecommunication carriers and enables companies determine what TFN was dialed.

An ACD can interpret the DNIS and route the call to an agent with a specific skill. This is called DNIS-based routing. Of course, customers need to know what TFN to dial for the service they need. This method is not practical for most businesses since it requires multiple 1-800 numbers rather than a single telephone number.

IVRs can eliminate this deficiency by offering customers a single telephone number for all services. As customers navigate the IVR script and select the skill they need, the IVR will automatically dial the TFN with a DNIS as if the customer called the TFN directly.

These routing methods work well when there are a limited number of ACDs to receive the TFN. However, this severely restricts the flexibility of your outsourcing solution by limiting the number of call centers that can be integrated.

Advanced features for in-cloud routing from your telecommunications carrier are another option. In-cloud routing can provide the ability to pre-route calls based on area codes, day-of-year routing, time-of-day routing, percentage call allocation routing, and other pre-defined programming.

## Intelligent Call Routing

A more sophisticated method uses **Intelligent Call Routing (ICR)**. ICR can integrate agents in multiple sites as a single virtual group, even if they are working from diverse outsourcers or from different ACDs.

ICR can evaluate conditions as they change and route calls to an optimum answering resource, such an IVR, agent, automated attendant, or voice mail—anywhere in the enterprise at any given moment. ICR programming looks at each incoming call and determines who is calling and why they are calling. The software can also combine call data with customer entered digits and/or information obtained from a customer profile database, if available.

Using this data ICR can deliver pre-populated screens of customer information, commonly known as screen pops, to decrease the average handle time and improve the quality of the agent-customer interaction.

## Post Routing Calls

ICR also has the ability for post-routing calls to a different agent or peripheral equipment, such as an ACD, PBX, or IVR. This enables a call to be rerouted from one agent to a different location or outsourcer.

ICR works best when connected to a Public Service Telephone Network (PSTN) Intelligent Network, typically abbreviated with the acronym IN. An IN is a service-independent telecommunications network in which intelligence is removed from the carrier switches and placed in computer nodes that are distributed throughout the carrier network.

When connected to a PSTN/IN, ICR solutions can re-route a call at the network level, avoiding the need for a single call to use both inbound and outbound lines. For example, if your caller elects to transfer from your IVR to an agent, you do not want to continue with the call connected to your IVR. This is called **hair-pinning** or **tromboning**, which means the caller continues to be routed through the IVR to talk to an agent. It is preferable to have the call disconnected from the IVR and reconnected to the agent. This commonly is known as **Take-back-N-Transfer, Transfer Connect,** and **Transfer and Release**.

If done effectively, these techniques reduce telecommunications costs and peripheral equipment resources while routing a customer call to the most available and qualified agent.

# 25 Establish Security Guidelines

**Security comes with a price, but without it, you risk an even higher cost.**

Security can be complex. It deals with user access to systems, data storage, Internet access, email retention, and many other operational processes. Yet, to a large extent, security for your call center work will be dependent on the network and operating systems established by your outsourcer. Hence, the need for guidelines.[18]

Guidelines should define the topics used in a basic checklist. The checklist should define physical and technical safeguards that protect the confidentiality, integrity, and availability of the electronic information that the outsourcer creates, receives, maintains, and transmits on behalf of your company from any anticipated threats, hazards, or improper access or use.

Guidelines need to reflect your own security goals and, likewise, used to evaluate the security of any prospective outsourcer. Keep in mind that you are already obligated to protect the confidentiality and integrity of your customers. Your outsourcer should honor the same commitment. Not providing guidelines may inadvertently violate contracts, expose confidential data, reduce market credibility, or result in government imposed penalties.

Security goals may vary, but at a minimum, your guidelines should incorporate policies to maintain the confidentiality of data, protection of data being modified by unauthorized sources, levels of access for applications and associated data, and accountability to verify compliance with security policies.

Outline enforceable security requirements in any contractual or other form of agreement. Remember these requirements have a lifecycle through which policies will be generated, applied, audited, and revised.

Validate your outsourcer has a **Chief Security Officer (CSO)**, or equivalent executive, that oversees security across their organization and periodically report on all aspects of security at his site.

Ensure your outsourcer has an organizational hierarchy that identifies who will have access to sensitive data or critical applications. Be sure you have established your own internal process for classifying data, and appropriate levels of security for each data class.

While your prospective outsourcer may independently submit the details of their security department in an RFP or other due diligence request, you should establish the security guidelines you expect to be followed. After all, it is your business.

As an example of what happens when guidelines are not enforced, consider the breach that Sony experienced between April 17 and April 19, 2011. After the breach, Sony informed the public that the names, addresses, and credit card numbers of 77 million of its users had been compromised.

Reuters later reported that Michael Pachter, Wedbush Securities Analyst, said "Sony probably did not pay enough attention to security when it was developing the software that runs its network. In the rush to get out innovative new products, security can sometimes take a back seat."[19]

Guidelines need to define the process of any new technologies, products, or data uses and identify the potential security impact, whether recommended by you or your outsourcer. Guidelines should also include the process for your outsourcer to respond to security "alerts" released by software vendors.

When security breaches are discovered, guidelines should set forth penalties and the procedures to correct the breach as promptly as possible.

Guidelines should stipulate an incident recovery/back-up plan, including backup software and a secondary site to maintain data, in case of any breaches in your information security systems. The guidelines should also mandate a process to eradicate data from equipment prior to disposal.

For the desktop, guidelines should mandate the use of virus protection programs and the regular updates of virus and software patches.

When guidelines are not followed, you will need to identify how to handle and resolve disputes. Thus, your guidelines need to include a plan for resolution of disputes arising out of security breaches or alleged misuse of customer identifiable information.

# 26 Promote a Security Culture

**Promoting a security culture requires a constant and consistent attitude to protect against malicious acts.**

Technical and physical guidelines are by no means the answer for all scenarios. It is essential to incorporate ethics into your guidelines. Establish policies for a "security culture" with your outsourcer through a formal training program for agents and call center staff to encourage outsourcer employees to follow the policies. Follow up the training periodically with classroom reviews, especially after a major breach has occurred anywhere in the industry to reinforce security principles.

Promoting a security culture requires a constant and consistent attitude to protect against malicious acts. That culture should start at the door with standardized electronic access devices that support secure entry to the building. Visitors should sign in, receive a temporary ID badge, and be escorted by an employee at all times. As employees and visitors perform their duties, every action at the outsourcer site should promote security awareness.

Of course, being able to promote a culture of security with your outsourcer makes the assumption that your company already has security guidelines you can provide your outsourcer.

If you don't have published guidelines, your company will need to dedicate a security staff to prepare the security policies and best practices. If staff is not dedicated, you need to feel confident they will have the time to develop the documentation and training materials. Moreover, when the occasion arises, your security staff will need the time to revise them. Training materials should be appropriate for educating all personnel levels on your policies. Materials should emphasize the importance of your security culture and the measures taken to enforce them.

At the foundation of the security culture, you must decide what data is sensitive and who should have access to such data. Implement a process for classifying data with appropriate levels of security for each data class. Include the methods for assigning and removing security levels to your outsourcer agents and support staff. Review how often their management reviews the policy and the annual budget dedicated to security tools and staffing.

The security guidelines you provide to your outsourcer may include numerous employee policies depending on your business, but at a minimum, they should include the procedures for hiring and termination. Hiring policies should require your outsourcer to perform background checks before hiring anyone handling sensitive customer information, such as financial, medical, or personal data. If the information handled by the outsourcer is proprietary, the policies should include a confidentiality statement signed by employees when they are hired. Employee qualifications regarding their technical abilities should also be verified to avoid security breaches due to an agent's or support personnel lack of technical ability.

Upon termination of employees or agents, outsourcer policies should ensure that access to facilities is changed and access to data is terminated.

During employment, you will need to enforce the culture with periodic audits to review security issues and ensure all outsourcer employees understand the importance of keeping sensitive customer information secure.

The security staff will require time to support security issues at the outsourcer site both proactively and as they arise. Schedule time to routinely audit the information security practices or systems to assure accurate execution of the policies and to assess vulnerabilities. Start the reviews when employees are hired. Then, perform periodic reviews regarding the use of data with appropriate senior managers and agent supervisors based on their position or function. Continuously monitor the access and use of data by the agents serving your customers.

Finally, your team will need to establish penalties for breaches of information security by agents and promptly implement them upon discovery of any information security issues.

# 27 Define Desktop Security for the Agents

**The outsourced agent desktop is where the most frequent security issues will occur.**

The outsourced agent desktop is where the most frequent security issues will occur. Agents can be adaptive and very ingenious when they want to find holes in your security to access social networks or take advantage of customer information. Although they understand your security rules, there will be numerous occasions when agents test the system. Many times this violation of security is done maliciously. But, even when the breach is harmless, it must be considered a security violation.

Proactively enforcing guidelines will help reduce this risk of a security violation through attention to policies, training, and culture. Management of your outsourcer must also be vigilant at all times and you must accept responsibility for the strict enforcement of guidelines.

Ultimately, the best approach to desktop security is to remove the ability of the agent to initiate any security breach. This is achievable using global desktop management. Since most agent desktops operate with Microsoft Windows, I will focus on those.

Microsoft offers technology that can manage a large number of computer and user accounts using Group Policy settings. These settings are contained in a **Group Policy Object (GPO)** that resides in a centralized model called **Active Directory (AD)** Services.

AD is an inverted tree-structure with containers. Containers identify users and computers with locations, domains, and organizational units

(OUs). By linking a GPO to an OU you can apply specific settings to all users and computers in that container.[20]

GPO can limit users to only have the minimum rights or privileges to perform their job. It can inhibit the agent's ability to save confidential data on local disk drives, network storage, or send it to an outside party from their desktop. When desired, GPO may restrict access to plug-in external drives, including flash drives, which are easily carried out of your building with huge amounts of information.

In addition to managing the desktop, agents should have limited access to only those Internet sites that are necessary to perform their required tasks. This restricts agents from using Internet websites for malicious purposes. Many Internet sites enable you to send articles to a friend or business associate with the ability to include a comment. While these Internet websites provide a helpful environment for many visitors to share news, they also provide an easy way for agents to send messages with confidential data that may be used for identity theft.

A common method to restrict access to only approved websites is to dictate the use of a whitelist or a blacklist. A whitelist is a set of Internet websites that agents are allowed to access. Conversely, a blacklist is a set of Internet websites that agents are *not* allowed to access and known to have undesirable content.

There are advantages and disadvantages to each approach. Whitelists only allow specific content but require constant maintenance for the ever-changing web. In contrast, there are well known companies that support blacklists, much like virus protection on your personal computer. Blacks constrain access to malicious websites, but may not restrict access to a website where messages with confidential data can be sent, such as a news website.

Either way, you need to know what your outsourced agents are accessing. Require your outsourcer to perform on-going monitoring and report on any security breaches of agents who manage to send data. Follow-up when breaches do happen and determine how it occurred and what impact it had.

Keep in mind that websites will continue to evolve with new techniques that promote information sharing. Agents will continue to use their ingenuity to find those new techniques. Consequently, you will need to proactively manage where the issues most frequently occur: at the desktop.

# 28 Reports Should Be Actionable

**Reporting needs to provide an objective source of performance measurement data.**

Outsourcing means you are going to allow other people to talk to your customers. How those people treat your customers will determine your reputation in the industry.

Knowing when your customer expectations are not being met can be determined through explicit and comprehensive reporting. However, call centers are people and data intensive. Thus, it is often difficult to identify and summarize the problems damaging your customer experience and their loyalty.

The difficulty may stem from gathering data from disparate sources that are tricky to integrate into a single view or from the complexity involved in interpreting the records into a meaningful summary.

Reporting may be on paper, through an extranet website, or on desktop dashboards. Reporting may be through real-time event notification sent via email when preset performance thresholds are exceeded. Whatever presentation methods are used, identifying what reports you need should be defined upfront with your outsourcer.

Online reporting can be global in content or highly personalized, such as reports for individual supervisor profiles with summaries that reflect performance data and metrics of every agent. Reporting may be tabular or graphical with the ability to be drilled down into daily detail or rolled up to any date range of week, month, quarter, or year. Since it is online, the information can be obtained in real-time, giving you or your outsourcer a continuous view of the center's performance and the ability to make better decisions—faster.

Consider an Intranet web-reporting tool for agents to view their personal statistics related to their team or line of business. This type of direct feedback is an excellent coaching tool that can show agents where their performance stands compared to their peers.

At a high level, reporting should include operations, efficiency, and quality monitoring. Operations and production reporting should capture inbound/outbound metrics and service levels that can be combined with financial data. Totals should be able to be aggregated from any combination of organizational levels, including manager, supervisor, team lead, line of business, or contact center in either summary or detailed format.

Efficiency reporting should provide detailed views of the way an agent manages time with key performance indicators to manage productivity from paid hours worked, occupancy rates, adherence to schedule, and show rates. Agent productivity reporting should include agent utilization, average handle time, wrap time, and exception reporting that tracks training and skills development or other time away from the system. You should be able to summarize agent activity, IVR activity, and queue information to spot trends and spikes as they emerge.

**Quality Assurance (QA)** reporting integrates agent effectiveness with scores from monitoring agent calls. QA performance reports can identify where agents are struggling, even where entire groups are faltering, across a line of business. Using a technique called drill-down, you can look into the data through recursive queries that can yield the details of a single call. As a result, the report results can be used to develop focused training that spotlights specific problems.

In summary, reporting needs to provide an objective source of performance measurement data for agent skill development, and coaching for any issues before it affects business objectives. It can provide a consolidated view of agent performance from systems that may include inbound call systems and dialers, payroll, time and attendance systems, and work force and case management platforms. It should provide metrics from every system that interacts with your outsourcer agents and helps improve the effectiveness of your outsourcer's call center strategies.

# 29 RFPs Are Only As Good As Your Requirements

**Ask your potential vendor to meet your business and technical requirements.**

A **Request for Proposal (RFP)** is an effective way for you to ask about a prospective outsourcer's solution and how it will satisfy your specific requirements and pick the right outsourcer.

Almost all companies use a RFP to select their outsourcer. Some companies create a **Request for Information (RFI)** to test their premise for outsourcing. RFIs enable you to get feedback on technical approaches for interfacing to your infrastructure and may yield differences in pricing from your original business and technical objectives. It will also enable you to prequalify companies for a RFP.

You may want to use a RFI to have prospective outsourcers submit their outsourcing approach in an open format with general questions. A RFI will require additional time to issue, respond to bidder's questions, obtain responses, and evaluate the submissions. You should allot about six weeks for the entire RFI process, but it may provide valuable insight into your RFP process and validate your assumptions.

Creating a RFP will require you to assemble all the business processes and technical requirements to be performed by your prospective outsourcer. Outline the objectives you want to accomplish in a clear and concise form. Describe the levels of service and performance that will be expected to ensure success. Equally important, define your technology objectives and outline how you expect their objectives to interoperate with yours.

A typical RFP contains an Executive Summary, Scope of Work, Functional Questions, Technical Questions, Organization Overview, and Pricing. The Executive Summary should provide a complete overview of the project with a summary of the objectives and the expectations of the proposed vendor.

The Scope of Work should provide additional details of your requirements. A complete work flow diagram is helpful for prospective outsourcers, including the identification of tasks you expect to perform. The scope should also define the methods your prospective outsourcer will need to access your customer data and application. Including this information will enable your bidders to provide better pricing on their tasks. When this information is not provided, pricing is usually higher to account for the unknown.

Include your Technical Questions about the technology the prospective outsourcer is proposing, including details of versions and capacities. Request their plan for version upgrades and their procedures for notifying you when scheduled.

Include your organizational chart with relevant personnel. Then, ask for the prospective outsourcer's organizational chart with equivalent technical and production personnel that would be assigned to your project. Request a brief biography of key personnel accomplishments. Request the name, title, and position of the executive to be assigned to your account and explain why this individual is appropriate for your business.

Request a proposed timeline with durations for critical tasks. This may need to be modified when a contract is rewarded, but it will provide insight to the bidder's experience in deploying a new call center.

Your RFP should require the prospective outsourcer to execute a **Master Services Agreement (MSA)** that includes specific terms of your arrangement, including performance metrics, service level credits, conditions for early termination, reporting, indemnification, and limitation of liability. Your agreement should require the prospective outsourcer to meet agreed upon service levels during the term of the agreement and specify penalties for the failure to achieve them.

Your RFP should also allow the prospective outsourcers the latitude to insert their best practices for achieving your objectives as well as respond to your specific needs. Remember that you are establishing the basis for a working relationship with the outsourcer and you will want to gain from their experiences.

Keep in mind that each response will be founded on the questions and information you provide in the RFP. Based on their answers and your due diligence, you will need to the proposed technology and personnel for the duration of your contract.

# The Devil Is in the Details

**The more specific the details you request, the better the response you will get.**

Your RFP should request sufficient details of the outsourcer facilities and technologies to provide a complete evaluation of each bid. These details may be requested in the form of questions to thoroughly understand the environment where your work will be performed. I provide the type of questions here to provide a high-level overview. These questions should not be interpreted as inclusive of all the items covered in a thorough RFP.

Questions should ask about the physical and environmental security policies where agents would be located. Ask if access to the building is controlled and if there is a data center on the premises, and is access to the computer room secured separately? Does the prospective outsourcer have other clients at the proposed facility and will there be dedicated seats in a separate area? Are all windows and doors electronically alarmed and with monitoring performed by an on-site or a third-party security company?

Inquire if third-party service providers or subcontractors are performing any segment of the outsourcing. These may be any external business entities that routinely receive, send, transmit, store, control, or process confidential or highly confidential information. Subcontractors may also be supplementing technology or supplying non-technology related services that involve handling your customer data. Each third party and the service being provided for the prospective outsourcer should be identified. You should also be sure the subcontractor has signed a non-compete/non-disclosure agreement that is applicable to the work being performed by the outsourcer.

Request the details of the prospective outsourcer's network topology. Most call center outsourcers serve multiple clients and will not share their entire network as it compromises the security of other clients. However, you should request a diagram of the network that will be used specifically for your outsourcing project. This should include the location of primary connection points with details of firewalls, routers, switches, and any DMZs.

You should request what types of devices are connected internally to the outsourcer's facilities and do they include wireless devices? Are the agents located at the outsourcer site or are they remote, such as work-at-home agents? If the agents are remote, how will secure access be enabled and monitored? If any information or services are provided by a third party, is it reflected in the network topology and are the connections secure?

Does the outsourcer have a set of policies and procedures regarding how data is accessed and stored? Questions should ask how the prospective outsourcer would report security incidents and denial of service attacks? Has antivirus software been deployed, updated, and maintained for all desktops, servers, firewalls, and Internet email gateways?

Does the outsourcer have restrictions that prevent confidential information, such as account numbers, from being sent externally through e-mail? Are there restrictions in place to prevent employees from accessing external e-mail servers? Are there policies or controls that restrict mobile phones and PDAs from being on the production floor?

Request what type of reporting the outsourcer will provide during the contract? Reports should include all metrics associated with call volume, including, but not limited to, average handle time, calls answered, calls abandoned, calls offered, and hold times.

Will the outsourcer provide a daily forecast of calls for the next business day? Will the outsourcer provide reports regarding employee attrition and future hiring plans to meet the call volume forecasts?

How will the quality of calls be managed? Will the outsourcer provide reports on the number and rating of calls monitored? Can the outsourcer provide remote access to the call recordings by your company to enable independent quality monitoring?

Ask about the outsourcer's business continuity and disaster recovery planning. Disasters happen and you need to ensure the availability of alternative processing services when normal processing is interrupted.

# 31 Go with Your Gut (and Some Analysis)

**There is never a clear winner when the best price is not the best value.**

Picking the right outsourcer is a combination of evaluating proposals, site visits, and independent background research on the outsourcers. Despite the critical nature of this process, many organizations underestimate the time and effort it takes to make a well-informed decision. Moreover, as you go through the outsourcer selection process, it is not uncommon to discover other requirements that may have been omitted in your RFP.

Making the decision can be done through a logical process, but in the end, selections are usually made from intuition and gut feel. However, there are some techniques you can use to validate your decision.

Evaluate each proposal based upon your understanding of how each proposal meets your objectives and satisfies your requirements.

Create an evaluation matrix that enables you to compare the responding companies against each other. Determine a weight on each requirement and a common scale to grade the response. This will enable you to emphasize the requirements that are important and give credit to requirements that may merely be nice to have. For each requirement emphasized, determine if each outsourcer has demonstrated the experience and efficiencies to ensure success.

Determine the cost for satisfying each requirement and evaluate the value for the price. There are no industry standards for pricing a service and not every outsourcer charges the same for the service. Keep in mind that pricing may not denote industry experience. Two outsourcers may price their service competitively, but one may have more experience and better customer skills and the ability to foresee problems and resolve issues faster.

Even if your operation requires domestic call centers, you may want to evaluate both on-shore and offshore locations. Your requirements may rely on domestic operations, but if price is a factor, then you should consider if your prospective vendor could service your needs offshore.

Part of your success will be dependent on the outsourcer's proposed technology. Understanding the technology offered is just part of the evaluation. You will need to evaluate your prospective outsourcer's ability to support not only prevailing technologies, but also technologies that are emerging and, as yet, unannounced. The ability to have your outsourcer keep pace with your technology advances is a key factor in a successful outsourcing relationship.

Distinguish the reputation of each prospective outsourcer. Your evaluation needs to go past the rhetoric and obtain each outsourcer's standing and experience through industry references.

Comprehend the financial strength of each outsourcing company; how long they have been in the business, and how they are organized? Some outsourcers are publicly trading companies and financials are readily available. Private vendors may not be willing to divulge their financials, so their experience with projects of similar nature is more important to your evaluation.

After you have identified your finalists, request an in-person presentation of their capabilities at the recommended call center site. On-site visits are a valuable way to get more information and evaluate the intangible aspects of a vendor.

These recommendations assume that your evaluation will be performed in a neutral environment with the latitude to freely make a decision. This is idealistic. Most vendor selection efforts are influenced by external factors such as management recommendations, purchasing decisions, or preferences through executive contacts.

The presence of these external factors does not mean that you should forgo the vendor selection process; however, it may mean performing your evaluation in a different light. At the extreme, these external factors can lead your team to an outsourcer that does not meet your business or technical requirements.

If such a case does arise, your evaluation matrix may become a huge asset. Complete the evaluation using the externally recommended vendor as a baseline and evaluate the other outsourcers accordingly. The resulting evaluation matrix will then enable you to make an argument for or against a specific course of action.

# 32 Know If the Outsourcer Is Outsourcing

**Does it matter if an outsourcer is subcontracting their proposed functionality?**

Outsourcing is a competitive business and providing services with aggressive pricing is always a critical factor in winning business. All companies look for methods to reduce their costs and outsourcers are no exception. To maintain their aggressive stance, outsourcers are following trends in the computer industry and using services in the cloud.

Cloud services are a by-product of the dot-com era. These services started as simple applications that could be shared over the Internet and have matured to challenge traditional client-server applications. An example is **Customer Relationship Management (CRM)** software. CRM is now offered in the cloud and referred to as **Software as a Service (SaaS)**. **SaaS** CRM has also spawned a number of companies that are adjuncts or directly interface with their solution.

**Infrastructure as a Service (IaaS)** is such as adjunct. IaaS offers in-cloud infrastructures such as ACDs (telephone switches), intelligently routing calls, outbound dialers, and voice and screen recordings. As a result, complete solutions for outsourcing inbound or outbound calls are available for a monthly fee.

Thus, it is essential to know if your potential outsourcer is outsourcing their technology. If they are, you will need to know to how to evaluate their capabilities. A vital question is, "If your outsourcer is using SaaS or IaaS, what value do they provide?"

The answer is dependent on how each outsourcing company integrates cloud computing into the services being offered to you. As in any approach, there are benefits and deficiencies of this technology. Your evaluation must determine if they meet your operational and technological goals and objectives. Here are some items to consider.

First, can the outsourcer demonstrate the effectiveness and reliability of the cloud computing solution being offered to you? The methods of the outsourcer may be presented as transparent to their operation and, indeed, your focus should be how your customers are treated and the effectiveness of the call center. Still, it is important to understand the technologies being used to fully evaluate the potential outsourcer.

Second, has the outsourcer added value to their cloud computing solution? **Platform as a Service (PaaS)** enables creation of value-added software to the solutions IaaS and SaaS offer. For example, using PaaS, the IaaS may log their transactions in the SaaS database. Another PaaS example is the integration of an IaaS user interfaces with a SaaS user interface. Hence, entering data to one user interface seamlessly enters the data into both solution databases.

SaaS and IaaS are typically offered over the Internet. Thus it is dependent on factors outside the control of the outsourcer. To overcome that issue, outsourcers with longstanding SaaS and IaaS vendor relationships may have implemented their own private network cloud. The private cloud ensures connectivity is being properly managed, especially when voice over internet protocols (VoIP) or session Internet protocols (SIP) has been integrated.

Third, if the potential outsourcer is using both SaaS and IaaS, what is the relationship between the companies? Many SaaS CRM vendors have developed a PaaS application-programming interface (API).

Fourth, is there a level of redundancy from the SaaS and IaaS vendors? Your potential outsourcer will be dependent on an infrastructure framework outside their control. Be sure your potential outsourcer can provide the details of the SaaS and IaaS vendor's business continuity plan.

Finally, if your outsourcer is using SaaS CRM or an IaaS vendor with your data or access to your data, stipulate who is responsible for the integrity and security of the data.

While these issues may appear as negative aspects of using cloud computing, there are also advantages. Data and business processes are not the domains of any outsourcer. As a result, outsourcing functions can easily move from one vendor to another. This inherent ability to easily change vendors may provide a significant advantage to your outsourcer strategy.

# 33 Perform Due Diligence on Subcontractors

**Will your outsourcer stand behind the quality of their subcontractors?**

If your prospective outsourcer does outsource any part of their operation, then there are some additional items you should include in your selection process. For the sake of clarity, I refer to companies supplementing your prospective outsourcer as third party service providers or subcontractors.

Again, subcontractors are any external business entity that routinely receive, send, transmit, store, control, or process confidential or highly confidential information. Subcontractors may supplement technology or supply non-technology related services that involve handling your customer data.

Evaluating how your prospective outsourcer will perform your work will require your company to develop a due diligence process. Due diligence should identify each service subcontracted along with the associated risk of using them. The risk should assess the criticality of each subcontracted service and the safeguards the prospective outsourcer has in place to ensure your business goals and objectives are met.

Due diligence should ensure the outsourcer has a unique contract for each subcontractor. These contracts should be available for your review on request to ensure the contract provides appropriate oversight of the services provided and appropriate language to securely maintain your data.

Your review should also include what monitoring mechanisms and processes relative to your stipulated service-level agreements are offered. The service agreement should include a clear specification of all-relevant terms, conditions, responsibilities, and liabilities of both parties. For example, the agreement should include: compliance, audit reporting, on-site review, notification of change/risk, SLAs, data ownership, insurance, liability, privacy, dispute resolution, problem reporting and escalation procedures, ongoing monitoring, and US Regulatory requirements.

If the contractor is a publicly owned company, your outsourcer should be aware of their process for researching, evaluating, and complying with all national and other laws and regulations that are relevant to the business, process, or activity being undertaken in the particular jurisdiction. This includes obtaining reasonable assurances the processes and procedures related to compliance with Sarbanes-Oxley regulatory requirements have been met. In addition you should know if the subcontractor reported any deficiencies.

You should also be aware of the country the subcontractor is operating in and if there are any country-specific regulations related to the products/services they provide. For example if the subcontractor is in the United States, they are required to comply with Federal Data Protection and the Health Insurance Portability and Accountability (HIPPA) Act.

Your due diligence should also identify how your prospective outsourcer will handle business continuity or recover from a complete outage at the subcontractor. This may include a centralized group, known as a **single point of contact** or **command center**, to gather incoming messages from the subcontractor regarding technology and operations. If there is a production impacting issue, the prospective outsourcer's command center should categorize and prioritize each issue. Your prospective outsourcer should define a pre-defined escalation path, which includes notification of your company.

Finally, it is tempting to believe that your prospective outsourcer will stand behind their commitments and manage the quality of their subcontractors. However, it would be prudent to implement a quality control process to make sure your customer's experience is high, their data secure, and back office support is performed accurately and completely.

# 34 Be Realistic about Implementation

**Things have taken longer than you thought and the timeline for a go live date is starting to look very short.**

If you are following the sequence of rules, the steps may have taken longer than you anticipated. After you determined your initial timelines, commitments were made to your executive management that were critical in obtaining their support. In all probability, the commitments included deploying on a date that seemed reasonable at the time in Rule 11, "Understanding Implementation Timelines," and perhaps even when you revalidated your schedule in Rule 19, "Validate Requirements."

However, your project has progressed and, if you are like most organizations, things have taken longer than you thought and the timeline for a go live date is in jeopardy. Moreover, there are sure to be objectives the business forgot to mention and questions the technology team didn't ask that might delay the timeline even further.

This is a critical milestone in your timeline and may be the last chance to reset expectations for a date to accept your first call. You will need to reassess the status of all dependent factors and develop a clear understanding of the time to complete your remaining tasks.

This is not to suggest your original dates were invalid. Everyone procrastinates. People assigned to your tasks get sidetracked with other projects and scope creep is always there. But now, you need to start putting stakes in the ground and establish realistic target dates. You may also have to defer business objectives or phase-in technology if not critical or identified as optional.

Appraise the timelines for business process changes against your outsourcer timelines. Ensure the timelines complement each other and do not leave holes in how your business operates when you go live.

Examine your outsourcer schedule for the preparation of their facilities. Make sure a separate area or a partial area will be available for training approximately four to six weeks prior to your go live date.

Walk through the steps to prepare your infrastructure. Do the same for your outsourcer. Include all the factors for interconnection such as network configuration, internal wiring, and carrier provisioning.

Be aware that both you and your outsourcer are dependent on dates provided by your long distance carriers. In turn, the long distance carriers are dependent on dates from the local exchange carriers for the last mile—on both ends of the circuit. Thus, carriers tend to provide conservative dates and getting a firm date for circuit installation that meets your schedule may be problematic.

Other scheduling should validate the time necessary to program the IVR. Dependent tasks should define how calls would be routed from the IVR options to the agents.

Sending calls to agents who are skilled differently may include intelligent call routing, as described in Rule 24, "Route the Call with Intelligence." If you are planning to use ICR, then allocate the time to program the ICR system and the time for your outsourcer to match the programming in their PBX/ACD.

If the outsourcer is going to access your data or applications, you will need to schedule time for your security team and your outsourcers to implement all the security policies for agents to access your data or applications without vulnerabilities. A subordinate task is to enable logins for agents to access them.

Obtain the tasks and schedule from your outsourcer to prepare for going live. This may include preparation on their PBX/ACD, setting up their local network, and configuring the desktop computers to meet your requirements.

Finally, detail the tasks that must be completed for your outsourcer to implement appropriate security measures in their facility. This should include controlled access to the area where your outsourcer's agents are located and video cameras in key locations of the outsourcer's facilities.

When you are complete, your schedule may have changed significantly. However, at this point, it should be realistic and provide the confidence to reset expectations for delivery.

# 35

# Review the Outsourcer Staffing Model

**There is nothing more important than hiring and developing agents. At the end of the day you are reliant on people, not strategies.**

Your outsourcer should have a plan for staffing, but you should approve it to be sure you are aligned with the approach.

An agent profile is critical for the outsourcer to begin the staffing process. Provide your outsourcer with an agent profile that includes the details of a job description for each agent skill or line of business.

If you do not have a profile, have your outsourcer complete one with the caveat that you need final approval of the profile to ensure it meets your business requirements. Integrate the profile into the talent management software used by your outsourcer.

## Talent Management Solutions

Talent management solutions are integral to how to select, manage, and retain agents. These solutions are capable of performing multiple assessments during the hiring process. As a result, you can obtain a complete candidate analysis that matches your agent profile. The candidate analysis can identify strengths and weaknesses, as well as gaps in skills and knowledge. Target agents with the ability to multi-task, navigate several different applications simultaneously, think logically, and do it all while maintaining a positive attitude.

The candidate analysis can also determine how well they can assimilate to your corporate culture. Understand that not everyone has the ability to be a good call center agent. The nature of the work is extremely repetitive, and it's just not the kind of job that most people are willing to commit to as a long-term career.

## Agent Training

The profile is also the foundation for training your outsourcer agents with the right skills to deliver world-class service. Agent preparation may range from basic customer service skills to advanced problem solving and recovery skills. Whatever the range, you need the confidence that the agent will be able to handle every situation, including calls with difficult customers. Be aware that most people do not remember what they learn in the classroom. Skill development needs time to simulate customer calls.

Provide your outsourcer with your training materials. The materials should structure an approach for handling customers in a variety of situations depending on the services contracted for. It should also include enhancement programs to keep agent performance high and provide avenues for possible advancement.

## Attrition

One of the objectives both you and your outsourcer should have is to minimize agent attrition, also known as annual turnover or the percentage of staffing lost that year. Agent development costs money and can reduce the performance of your outsourcer if attrition is high. Moreover, agents who stay for even a few years can make a dramatic difference in performance and results.

## Work Force Management

Developing a accurate staffing model is almost impossible without a **Work Force Management (WFM)** system. The challenge for creating a staffing model is to determine how many seats are required to meet your project call volumes and creating an effective agent schedule; both while minimizing your costs for operations.

Your call volumes will continually change as may your hours of operations. Each may vary on a number of factors including season, special sales, holidays, and time zones. Moreover, even if the number of seats is accurately forecasted, your outsourcer still needs to be sure they can schedule agents to fill them.

To track if those seats are occupied, validate your outsourcer is using a WFM with the ability to provide the staffing schedule to meet your forecasted call volume. Ensure their WFM solution can also generate standard reports to track agent performance by skill, by line of business, or by individual agent.

# 36 Stay Involved in Real-Time

**Work with the outsourcer agents as if they were your own.**

Plan to work with the outsourcer agents as if they were your own. Start by setting your expectations for the agents. Obviously, the most important expectation is for your outsourcer to provide courteous service to your customers and effectively respond to all calls in a professional manner, which is a function of quality monitoring. The next expectation you need to establish is standards for agent performance during your hours of operation. To ensure your agents meet these expectations, monitor your performance metrics in real-time.

There are no industry standards that make sense for all industries. Different industries have different expectations for customers waiting in queue, average handle time, or transfers to different agents.

No matter what performance metrics are used, inbound call centers operate at the whim of the customer. This means agent performance is subject to the dynamic flow of call volume that may be affected by the time of year, campaign advertisements in the media, or pertinent news events. Thus, you need real-time monitoring to stay involved.

Monitoring operations in real-time is a task that everyone wants, but few companies actually accomplish. At a high level, real-time monitoring is the continuously gathering, analyzing, reporting, and alert notifications on the performance of voice communications, data networks, security measures, and agent productivity. At a detailed level, it can help to determine when an agent is struggling to resolve caller issues and needs targeted training and coaching.

It is not possible to catch every issue, every time. Nevertheless, being able to review your operations in real-time will improve your ability to spot issues and quickly apply corrective action.

One method of continuously monitoring is through the use of dashboards, which I note in Rule 28, "Reports Should Be Actionable." Dashboards can provide a continuous view of your operation interrelations. For example, displaying wait times against call volumes can enable you to perform a quick diagnosis that points to potential issues with staffing levels.

Real-time dashboard monitoring can track call statistics such as agent utilization rate or occupancy, average speed of answer, and abandonment rate. It may also provide the symptoms of more serious technical issues inhibiting agent performance. For example, a dashboard can display the rate of abandonment or the percentage of calls disconnected before an agent picks it up. This may be a staffing issue or it may denote a potential problem with voice circuits. The point is that if customers are hanging up in high numbers, then something is wrong and you need to become involved.

Dashboards aren't the place for deep analysis or introspection. They provide a simple presentation of data in a short period of time to react to a current situation.

Real-time monitoring also involves human intervention. Even the best of systems can alert you to every issue. Moreover, not all issues have the same impact on operations and finding a way to communicate this relative importance is valuable. Perhaps the best way is in a Command Center, which I describe in Chapter 39, "Communicate When Technology Breaks."

But, whatever method you use to monitor operations, the essential component is you. Stay involved in every aspect to ensure your outsourcer agents and their supporting systems achieve optimum performance.

# 37 Monitor Customer Satisfaction in All Media

**The customer is always right.**

Monitoring customer satisfaction, commonly referred to as CSAT, will provide additional metrics that will help you understand how your outsourced agents are performing in terms of service, quality, and efficiency.[21]

CSAT metrics have traditionally focused on voice communications. However, new methods for interfacing with your customers, such as email, chat, and social media require a new perspective on the traditional metrics to appraise how your outsourcer is performing and whether your customers are truly satisfied with their service.

### Service

The most important CSAT metric is service and it is equally as important with new media as it is with voice. Service includes measurements such as blockage, abandon rates, service levels, and the average speed of response.

Blockage is common to all media and defined as the percent of contacts not allowed to connect to an agent over the total contacts received. Voice blockage may include busy signals, carrier messages, or forced disconnects from trunks at total capacity. Data blockage for new media can occur in chat sessions when there is a shortage of bandwidth or when an email cannot be delivered. Although the reasons for blockage are different, the net effect is the same: customers become frustrated with the inability to reach your agents.

Service also measures the number of abandons in media connections. The rate of abandonment can be the result of technical blockage, a high volume of calls/chats, or just the tolerance of callers waiting for an available agent. While abandonment may not be entirely under your outsourcer's control, it does affect your customer experience and needs to be held to a minimum.

Service level is another measurement defined as the percentage of calls or chat requests answered within a set number of seconds; for example, 80 percent of contacts answered in thirty-five seconds no matter if voice or chat.

Social media is a little more tolerant according to a study of restaurant responsiveness on Facebook performed by Expion.[22] In this study, the average response time was six hours thirty-four minutes for 28 percent of all messages received on a brand's Facebook wall.

The longest acceptable response times are still email, but there are still industry acceptable response times. For example in a study of email responses at Amazon, responding in twenty-four hours would fail to meet the expectations of 40 percent of customers.[23]

## Quality

The second category is quality. Quality includes measurements such as first call resolution rate, transfer rate, communications etiquette and adherence to procedures.

The foremost measurement is the rate of FCR for customer satisfaction as I have previously discussed. Another is transfer rate defined as the percentage of calls/chats transferred to another agent divided by the total. No one likes to be transferred and restate his or her issue to a new agent. If the transfer rate for a contact is excessive, then it is likely the call routing rules need to be modified or agents need additional training.

Measuring communications etiquette and adherence tend to be subjective and should be rated by trained personnel. Trained personnel can numerically score the contact based on pre-determined business criteria to determine how an individual agent and the operation as a whole perform.

## Efficiency

Efficiency includes indicators of how well your outsourcer agents are being used. It is important as a gauge of the outsourcer effectiveness, and CSAT. Average Handle Time (AHT) is an indicator of performance, measuring how long it takes an agent to handle a customer issue. For voice, AHT is usually the amount of talk time plus after call work (ACW). Chat and email AHT is more difficult to gauge and may be measured as completed customer interactions per hour or day.

Additional metrics are numerous, and not all metrics may apply to your business. However, CSAT should always be foremost. How you do it is not as important as what you do to measure it and whether it reflects the satisfaction level of your customers.

# 38 Monitor Call Quality

**Monitoring should be about identifying and amplifying positive messages.**

Call quality monitoring is essential for any contact center. It provides insight into how your outsourcer agents are performing and what your customers are really experiencing.

To perform call monitoring, your outsourcer should use a single system for recording all types of media used in the customer interaction including phone calls, email, or text chat. Using a single system can provide a 360-degree view of the customer interaction including all of the agents who interacted with them, regardless of media.

If you have not considered audio recording, consider that fines against call centers are becoming more common, especially in heavily regulated industries. If you or your outsourcers do not follow regulatory guidelines, you may have difficulty proving agents were compliant. As a result, you may be subject to nuisance lawsuits in which your customers threaten to file a complaint with the hope you will pay them off for not reporting regulatory transgressions.

Aside from regulatory requirements, the benefits of monitoring go beyond listening to calls on an ad-hoc basis to grade agent performance. It can be used to set standards for process improvement, coaching, and agent development.

The percentage of calls you want recorded depends on your specific requirements. However, industry trends are 100 percent recording of audio and partial recording of screens.

Audio recordings are typically maintained from two months to six months, unless there are regulatory requirements that stipulate longer durations or a unique business justification. Screen recordings that enable synchronized playback with audio recordings are storage intensive and the disk requirements to keep files for extended periods are expensive. Thus, screen recordings are typically only kept for several weeks, since they merely capture agent screens and not the interaction of both parties.

## Quality Evaluations

Quality evaluation is only as good as the person doing the evaluating. You and your outsourcer need to maintain a dedicated team of specialists with the resources, skills, coaching, and training to perform the monitoring. Supervisors are there to manage the agents and call escalations, not to monitor quality. By giving that role to a dedicated individual or team, you leave your supervisors free to manage.[24]

When initiating a monitoring program, there may be a tendency for agents to believe it will be used as a critical process against them. Alternatively, if your outsourcer previously had a monitoring system in place for a long time, agents may take it for granted.

Monitoring agent calls needs to be promoted as a positive activity and an integral part of the improving agent skills and improving customer relationship. It should not be advertised as a program to catch agent errors or used to demote agent performance. Rather, it needs to be collaborative rather than prescriptive and inclusive rather than authoritarian to promote acceptance and cooperation.

Feedback to the agent should be objective using a consistent method of scoring and evaluating that is fair and agreed by all in advance. Once methods are agreed and set, they must be maintained, built upon, and improved. Feedback may be delivered one-to-one, remotely, or in a team meeting where 'good' or 'unsatisfactory' are presented. Whatever method is selected, the important thing is that there is an opportunity for agents to contribute to the discussion. Such participation encourages agent buy-in and makes them feel their input is valued and that your team culture is inclusive.

Agent participation is also a good way to maintain best practices and ensure agents understand how to deal with customers using positive phases throughout the call. Regular quality monitoring prevents bad habits spreading from agent to agent, supports feedback for training, and maintains high customer satisfaction.

Lastly, reward high-quality work through methods such as 'agent of the month' awards, staff excellence certificates, or an acknowledgement in your outsourcer newsletter. If your customers are pleased with an agent's performance, pass it on.

# Communicate When Technology Breaks

**Yesterday it worked Today it doesn't Technology is like that Why is anyone surprised?**

The technology to implement call centers is becoming increasingly sophisticated. Not only is it more complicated to implement, but it is also more complex to maintain. While newer technology is more reliable and resilient, it should not be surprising that from time to time, technology breaks. The reasons why technology breaks are numerous, but when it does, one of best ways to maintain communication with your outsourcer is through a Command Center, both theirs and yours.

A command center can be the best method for gathering information, routing relevant data to decision-makers, and publishing summaries of action taken. It is also where business and clients interact with operations and IT.

Command centers should be staffed with agents that don't just operate with a set of procedures when issues occur. They need the ability to analyze issues, continuously interact with technical engineers, moderate technical bridges, and escalate when the issue demands.

Over time, the staffs of both your command center and that of your outsourcer will get to know each other. Staffs will know the folks they interact with as individuals, understand their idiosyncrasies, and have a pretty good handle on day-to-day operations.

The role of each command center is to gather incoming messages from all sources: technology, operations, business managers, and each other. If the message is related to a production impacting issue, the action should be categorized and prioritized. The centers should interface with information technology specialists and business managers to optimize decision-making and determine if further action is required. This enables critical issues to receive the attention they need in a timely manner and minimize any impact to customer service.

The mission of your command center may best be described as performing three vital tasks.[25]

**Communication and Intelligence** to effectively communicate and receive information from all sources including operations, technology, and business managers. For critical issues, one of the best ways of communicating in real-time is through the use of a conference call or "bridge." Conference bridges should use trained moderators that can facilitate the collection of data and prompt engineers to determine an appropriate course of action.

For issues that are not critical, the command center should publish periodic communications that provide updates and the time of resolution.

**Command and Control** that immediately implements the collective recommendations of the conference bridge for critical issues and submits work orders for resolution of other issues. As part of this function, the command center should have a process that escalates issues when they age to a predefined threshold. For example, urgent issues may be escalated after thirty minutes; high issues may be escalated after sixty minutes; medium issues may be escalated after four hours; and low issues may be escalated after a day.

**Coordinate and Document** the actions taken in response to an event including time, the individual taking the action, and the command center staff logging the action.

Command centers are only as effective as their tools. Your Command Center, and those of your outsourcers, should use the same software for trouble ticket management with the ability to exchange information on common events.

Choosing the right software should be properly researched. There are a variety of software packages for managing trouble tickets available commercially and a few good freeware solutions. Whatever solution you select, it should have a few key features. It should email command center staff, business managers, and technology managers as soon as a new case or trouble ticket is entered into the system.

Command centers need to monitor all aspects of operations. When issues do occur, your outsourcer should provide a root cause analysis detailing the issue, the impact, the times, and the recommended corrective actions. The root cause should be swift and within a maximum of seventy-two hours to correct any issues, avoid future failures, and recommend technology or operational improvements to increase reliability.

# 40 | Things Change

**Change corrects the objectives the business forgot to mention and enables solutions the technology team forgot to include.**

Markets, products, and customers change in business. So do the systems that support how agents service your customers. Change is inevitable and how to manage that change is an important segment of your outsourcing process.

Managing change ensures that modifications to any part of the technology, business process, and/or operations are introduced in a controlled and coordinated manner. It also minimizes the risk that unnecessary or unexpected changes are not introduced into your outsourcer's or your own operations.

Change control is a management discipline and follows a flow of activities recommended by organizations such as the **IT Infrastructure Library (ITIL)** that describes Best Practices in IT services.[26]

At a high level, successful change control follows these steps:

1. Documenting the reason for the change
2. Performing an impact assessment of the change
3. Obtaining approval of the change and the procedure to implement the change
4. Defining test procedures
5. User acceptance

The need for change may come from any number of conditions. Change may stem from the need for new functionality, the identification of a problem, or an upgrade to an existing system.

Change control also has a degree of flexibility to remedy a production impacting issue, which needs to be handled much differently than major changes with expanded project plans. Whether the change is immediate or long term, you and/or your outsourcer need to perform an impact assessment of the change.

If an immediate change is necessary to maintain production, then, at a minimum, a peer-to-peer review of the proposed change and review after the change is recommended. Two views of a problem are always beneficial and a quick peer-to-peer review can alleviate many unexpected results.

If the modification is more substantial, then a more detailed assessment should be made. This requires a thorough description of the change including an overview of the components impacted, the technical resources necessary to make the change, and the steps involved in implementation. The assessment should also include the testing necessary to ensure the change has been made correctly and how to back-out the change if it is not successful.

The assessment should be published to all departments for a complete review. Obtain approval from all parties and note the exceptions. As you review the assessment, keep in mind that outsourcers tend to share resources to minimize their costs. An ACD used to answer calls for your agents may also be used to answer the calls of another company. Thus, you should review all changes from the outsourcer to ensure a change for another client will not impact yours.

When changes are scheduled, open a conference bridge and invite the stakeholders and participants to join. It is also good practice to invite your command centers to serve as moderators for the change. The command center should take notes, detailing the steps and times for future reference. If something should go awry with the implementation, the command center is your best instrument to escalate the issue.

Before the change, perform a test of the functionality and benchmark the results. After the change, testing should be performed to ensure that technology operates in the same manner. If you have enabled new functionality, test all affected components to ensure all systems are operational. Either way, all parties should agree that the change has been implemented correctly and the expected results achieved.

If the results are not as expected, you will need to determine if a rollback to the previous state is required. If a rollback is performed, test again to be sure that everything is working as it was prior to the change.

In summary, change management should be used whether a change is necessary to repair a simple, immediate production issue or if major upgrades are in long-term planning. Either way, you avoid the issues of unexpected results when things change.

# 41

# Disasters Happen

**What to do when the lights go out.**

It doesn't matter where your outsourcer site is located; it is at risk of a disaster. That disaster may be from a utility outage, storm, flood, fire, quake, volcano, or act of violence. Moreover, disasters usually don't happen as a single event. They involve multiple facets. For example, storms may involve flooding or heavy snow with the loss of electricity and/or communications

No matter what the disaster, you and your outsourcer need to have a plan for business continuity and disaster recovery. The plan should pre-define what personnel will do to reestablish operations during an emergency at your outsourcer facilities.

Even as you plan, these pre-defined procedures should not to be interpreted as the only course of action. In most cases, they should be overshadowed by common sense or modified by the conditions of the particular emergency. Also recognize your planning will not remain static. You will need to amend your planning to reflect changes in your operations and that of your outsourcer.

As you plan, recognize that disasters have different levels of severity: minimal loss, partial loss, and complete loss.

**Minimal loss** can be a temporary loss of a utility such as water, electrical, or communications. It may also be a weather-related closure without damage to facilities or loss of staff. In a minimal loss scenario, there may be little to do but work with the utilities or wait for the weather. If the loss impacts operations for more than a day, you need to have a plan for an alternative site with the ability to take the calls for the stricken site.

Planning should be part of your outsourcer selection. Pick one site in a warm southern climate and another in the northern climate, because hurricanes and snowstorms rarely happen at the same time.

If your outsourcer is offshore, be sure their site has alternative power supplies such as an uninterruptable power supply and generators. An alternative water supply is also good planning since facilities without water can be just as disruptive as a lack of electricity.

Minimal loss planning should include the impact of pandemics such as the avian flu, SARS, and other unpublicized diseases. For example, in 2009, The World Health Organization estimated the global H1N1 (swine flu) outbreak could infect 2 billion over the course of the pandemic.[27] The flu may not be destructive to your outsourcer's call center, IT systems, or facilities, but they can a severe impact on your workforce.

Planning for pandemic emergencies should provide the option for agents to work at home to prevent the spread of infection. You will need to plan for the shift in network loads for agents who remotely login and an alternate means of voice communications to continue normal call flow.

**Partial loss** of a physical location requires planning to reorganize the work. Planning for a partial loss is similar to a minimal loss scenario except that you need to deal with damage to facilities. Recovering from a partial loss may mean moving agents to an undamaged portion of the building, but emphasis should be to the safety and well-being of personnel.

**Complete loss** denotes the full destruction of a call center site and equipment. Planning for a complete loss requires the relocation of operations for an indefinite period of time while reconstruction of the facility is performed.

Detailing the action for each of these levels is sufficient for planning. However, to ensure that plans can be invoked when actual disasters happen requires testing. Disaster recovery testing determines how well you have planned and requires a heavy investment in time and manpower. If the test doesn't work, your teams must find the flaw and retest. Thus, you and your outsourcer should recognize the resource commitment to configure networks and communications for the test and to return the configuration to its normal state.

# 42

## These Are My Rules. What Are Yours?

The rules I have outlined cover much of what is necessary to plan the outsourcing of your call center. Those who are experienced in call center outsourcing know there is much more detail than what I have provided herein. For those who are new to the world of outsourcing, I hope these rules have provided some insight into the tasks necessary to succeed.

It is also necessary to remind the reader that rules do not provide an exact strategy to follow, but rather guidelines to provide a general direction. Nothing is black and white in this industry. The call center business is dynamic, sometimes requiring rapid changes in strategy, technology, and operations necessary to respond to market conditions. For example, consider the impact that social media is about to have on customer service.

If you are outsourcing your call center, you are going to find new rules that are applicable for prescribing your business requirements or preferred techniques. These rules may be unique to your business or applicable to an industry. Either way, they are your rules with the potential to become proven tactics.

My rules include developing an outsourcing strategy, evaluating and selecting an outsourcer, understanding your technology options, identifying your risks, and on-going management. However, there may be many other rules that may be necessary for you to meet your specific requirements.

For example, your rules might include an on-site analysis of your prospective outsourcers, managing shifts in business objectives during your implementation, developing agent profiles, defining the hiring procedures, training the trainer, deploying the first wave of agents, and preparing for your first go live call. Your rules may also include the rules for transitioning from another outsourcer or changing your case management systems.

Understanding the order of the rules is as important as the rule itself. I have attempted to define my rules in a logical order, sequencing each rule from the activities of previous rules or positioning the rule appropriately. Some of these rules may apply in parallel. For example, determining what your technical and business objectives are should precede defining what to ask for in your RFP.

The best rules are going to come from your own experiences. As anyone experienced in the industry can attest, outsourcing a call center provides a wealth of experience, knowledge, and good stories. This experience may help you define new rules. Once you have defined your rules, determine where each rule fits into your business process workflow. Do your rules have prerequisites or other rules that must be performed prior to your particular activity? Is your new rule a prerequisite for another activity?

Define what will make the activities of your rule a success, describe the lessons learned from your experience, and identify the items to avoid. Remember that sometimes, knowing what not to do is just as meaningful as your recommendations about what to do.

Ultimately, my rules will not guarantee success and neither will yours. Rules will help improve your customer's experience, manage your risks, and improve your overall opportunity for success when outsourcing your call center.

**Planning the Implementation Strategy**

The implementation strategy defines the general approach for the solution implementation. The intent of the implementation strategy is to identify what is necessary to establish a framework of activities with the roles and responsibilities of both your organization and your outsourcer.

The strategy should also identify the questions you expect the outsourcer to address in a Request for Proposal (RFP)

### Scope of Implementation

- Is this a complete outsourcing of the call center or a partial outsourcing?
- If a complete outsourcing, what business areas will be impacted?
- If a partial outsourcing, will calls be sent as overflow from any type of call or for a specific line of business?

### Inter-communications

- What roles will be necessary for maintaining communications between your business and the outsourcer?
- What methods of communication will be used?

### Business Process Reengineering

- Will business process re-engineering be required?
- Will new policies be required?

- If the solution requires staff reorganization, how will staff positions be converted and/or established?

## Infrastructure Preparation

- What roles will be needed by both your team and the outsourcer to prepare the technology infrastructure?
- How many sites will need to be connected to the infrastructure?
- What is the maximum number of agents that should be located at each site?
- Will the solution use any of your existing technology infrastructures?

## Data Access

- Will the outsourcer need access to an existing database or will a copy need to be replicated at their site?
- If access is provided to your database,
    - How will user access be controlled?
    - What tools will be necessary at the outsourcer desktop?
    - How will updates be monitored for auditing?
- If replicated at the outsourcer site,
    - How will they convert the data to the new database at their site?
    - Will data validation and cleansing be necessary?
    - How much conversion will be automated?
    - What tools will they need to ensure data is synchronized?

## Call Center Deployment

- If the solution is implemented across the country or across the world, how will it be rolled out?
- Will there be "big bang" or incremental deployment? If incremental, what are the criteria for deciding the order in which call center sites will be deployed?
- If a solution, or vendor, is being replaced, how will the operations be switched over? Will there be a pilot operation?
- Will there be a time of parallel operation? If so, how long?

## Training

- What roles will your team and the outsourcer need for training?
- What topics are in the training class syllabus?
- How many people should be trained in each class?
- Is any specialized training needed?

## Change Management

- What roles will your team and the outsourcer need for implementing changes?
- What process will track changes?

## Change Request

- How will changes to the implementation plan be submitted and approved?
- How will changes to the system be submitted and approved?

## Problem Resolution

- What roles will your team and the outsourcer need by for problem resolution?
- What is the escalation process for technical issues?
- What is the escalation process for business issues?

## Help Desk Procedures

- What roles will your team and the outsourcer need for help desk services?
- What is the expected response time or Service Level Agreement?

# Life Cycle Methodology for Call Center Outsourcing

Life Cycle methodology models describe the activities within a project phase and the interrelationships between them. Because the steps of a methodology model are described in very general terms, the models are adaptable and their implementation details may vary among different organizations. Organizations may mix and match different life cycle models to develop a model more tailored to their products and capabilities.

A methodology model depicts the significant activities of call center outsourcing from strategy definition until going-live. It specifies the relationships between project phases, including transition criteria, feedback mechanisms, milestones, baselines, reviews, and deliverables. Typically, a life cycle model addresses the following phases of an outsourcing project: conceptual objectives and strategy definition, detailed requirements specification, design and implementation, and deployment and support. Much of the motivation behind utilizing a life cycle model is to provide structure to avoid the problems of the "undisciplined approach."

Critical components to the methodological approach are the knowledge of:
- People, structure, and functions of the call center organization
- Processes and procedures to be outsourced and the benchmarks used to measure success
- Technology used to support the outsourcer
- Business strategy at the operational level

The methodology model presented here is based on a four-phase approach that includes:

- **Phase 1: Conceptual Objectives and Strategy Definition** with an extended corporate vision that is critical to a comprehensive consistent implementation of an outsourced call center
- **Phase 2: Detailed Requirement Specifications** includes a statement of requirements to meet the objectives of the outsourcing
- **Phase 3: Design and Implementation** enables the technology, agent staffing, and quality monitoring to be implemented with tangible results
- **Phase 4: Deployment and Support** evaluates the deployment and potential incremental improvements to add value and ensures the outsourcing is consistent with the corporate vision

## Phase 1—Conceptual Vision and Strategy Definition

Phase 1 of the methodology defines the end-state vision of the outsourced solution, establishes the goals and objectives of project, and sets the groundwork for the next steps. This phase should:

- Evaluate current business requirements for outsourcing
- Validate business goals and objectives
- Identify the technology and products to meet the business goals and objectives
- Determine the level of difficulty and risk to implement the solution to outsource your call center
- Define the end-state solution including all aspects of the outsourcing process

## Phase 2—Detailed Requirement Specification

Phase 2 of the methodology occurs after the acceptance of the end-state vision of the outsourced solution. This phase should develop a detailed design of the solution including a definition of the requirements to meet both the technical and business goals and objectives. It should also define the necessary technology the outsourcer should provide.

The phase should provide the following:

- Detail the technology requirements for your internal solution
- Detail the technology requirements for your outsourcer
- Identify new technology to be purchased
- Identify the existing technology that needs to be updated
- Project call volumes and determine your busy hour
- Assess and revise call flows that will go to the outsourcer
- Assess operational changes in your organization
- Assess agent requirements
- Develop escalation procedures and business continuity requirements
- Develop impact analysis of the outsourced processes with associate risks

## Phase 3—Design and Implementation

Phase 3 of the methodology occurs after the acceptance of the detailed requirements by both your business and technology management. The phase should use the detailed requirements to design and implement both technical and operational procedures for the outsourcer to handle your call flow.

The phase should provide the following:
- Finalize the technology design for your internal and outsourcing solution
- Document operational procedures to meet the outsourced environment
- Identify the technical and business expectations for your outsourcer
- Document a request for proposal to select a qualified outsourcer
- Select an outsourcer
- Finalize requirements and coordinate planning to go live
- If the outsourcer is proposing an unprepared site, then determine the tasks, associated resources, and timelines for:
  - Developing a suitable floor plan to meet your ramp plan
  - Ordering the agent cubicles, chairs, and carpeting to build out the area to your specifications
  - Ordering the desktop computers, telephones, voice, and data communication equipment necessary for the initial group of agents to be deployed
  - Preparing the production floor for occupancy
  - Wiring the production site for telecommunications and network to the desktop
- Review the outsourcer training curriculum
- Monitor the hiring and training process
- Implement the technology to send calls to your outsourcer

For voice communications, determine the tasks, resources, and timelines to:
  - Order circuits and Toll Free Numbers (TFN)
  - Program your Interactive Voice Response system with options for your outsourcer
  - Configure call routing based on your business objectives
  - If you are using standard voice, test voice connectivity to your outsourcer PBX/ACD
  - If you are using VoIP/SIP, test voice connectivity to the agent desktop

For data communications, identify the task, resources, and timelines to:
  - Order data circuits
  - Mutually agree on an IP addressing scheme for your outsourcer to access your applications. This may require establishing rules to NAT (Network Address Translation) your IP addresses to the scheme used by your outsourcer.
  - Engineer and deploy networking components including firewalls and security policies

- Test application connectivity to the desktop
- Implement the technology to monitor technology and agent performance
- Test the entire process from receiving a customer call to routing the call to an agent desktop in your outsourcer sites
- Establish a go live date

## Phase 4—Deployment and Support

The process to go live and support the solution is dependent on the implementation of technology and the readiness of your outsourcer to accept calls. Prior to going-live you will need to

- Visit the outsourcer site and assess readiness
- Review outsourcer management and supervisors at the site
- Assess agent training curriculums and ensure they are being followed
- Assess agent readiness with your outsourcer

Going-live on Day One is an exciting time and validates your planning, design, and implementation in a single moment. Redirecting that first call to your outsourcer may seem to be the end, but there are more tasks to do before you can call the outsourcing a success. These include

- Monitor calls to ensure the agent is responding appropriately
- Perform thorough quality assurance from voice and/or screen recordings
- Review call statistics with your outsourcer
- Identify agents and supervisors requiring remedial training

The final step in the process is to maintain technology and continue process improvement. In the last step, you increase awareness of the technology in your organization, support your outsourcer in their technology, and evaluate success and opportunities for improvement.

# IVR Best Practices

**IVR Best Practices** are an accumulation of methods that can be employed to provide the IVR caller with the best possible experience while engaged with the telephone system. This is a fine balance between providing the information and transactional result that the organization requires while satisfying the needs of the caller. Implementation of these best practices should be performed using a systems approach for the design and development of IVR applications, which include, but are not limited to:

1. Providing callers with a maximum of four options per menu from which to choose, with the most frequently selected options being first in the list.
2. Allowing callers to key ahead for quickly navigation through the IVR menus.
3. Ensuring keypad presses are consistent throughout the entire IVR experience.
4. Describing the key action first, followed by the key to press.
5. Allowing callers to talk with an agent with the understanding that not all caller needs can be satisfied by an IVR system.
6. Employing a single voice for all menu prompts for consistency of presentation.
7. Using prompts that are natural sounding and easy to understand.
8. Testing the IVR for success factors prior to implementation.
9. Measuring caller acceptance before, during, and after implementation.
10. Creating a test system before it goes live to fine tune the full implementation.
11. Advising callers of planned changes in advance.

12. Providing ongoing monitoring of the IVR to ensure user acceptance.
13. Performing IVR load testing with adjunct systems to ensure a high concurrent volume does not impact the caller experience.
14. Developing an effective contingency plan if the IVR fails.

# D Assessing Security[28]

### 1. Maintaining a Secure Network

### 1.1 Maintaining a Firewall

1. Are your outsourcer's routers, switches, wireless access points, and firewall configurations secured and do they conform to your security standards?
2. Do changes to their firewall need change control and are the changes logged?
3. Is a firewall used to protect the network and limit traffic to agents?
4. Are egress and ingress filters installed on all border routers to prevent impersonation with spoofed IP addresses?
5. Is customer information stored in a database located on the internal network, not the DMZ, and protected by a firewall?
6. Do mobile/laptop computers with direct connectivity to the Internet have a personal firewall and anti-virus software installed?
7. Are Web servers located on a publicly reachable network segment separated from the internal network by a firewall (DMZ)?
8. Are firewalls configured to translate (hide) internal IP addresses, using network address translation (NAT)?

### 1.2 Vendor-supplied defaults for system passwords and other security parameters

1. Are vendor default security settings changed on production systems before placing the system into production?
2. Are vendor default accounts and passwords disabled or changed on production systems before they are placed into production?

3. Are all production systems (servers and network components) hardened by removing all unnecessary services and protocols installed by the default configuration?
4. Are secure, encrypted communications used for remote administration of production systems and applications?

## 2. Protecting Client information

### 2.1 Protecting stored client information

1. Are procedures in place for customer information to be securely disposed of when no longer needed?
2. Are all but the last four digits of the account number or social security number masked when displaying a customer's personal information?
3. Are account numbers and social security numbers (in databases, logs, files, backup media, etc.) stored securely—for example, by means of encryption or truncation?
4. Are account numbers and social security numbers sanitized before being logged in the audit log?
5. Is all your customer information stored and processed by your outsourcer directly and not available to sub-contractors?

### 2.2 Encrypt transmission of client information across public networks and wireless networks

1. Are transmissions of client information encrypted over public networks through the use of SSL or other industry acceptable methods?
2. If SSL is used for transmission of customer information, is it using version 3.0 with 128-bit encryption?
3. Is your outsourcer able and willing to set up TLS between their e-mail server and your e-mail server for encrypting all e-mail between the organizations?

### If your outsourcer uses wireless technology:

1. Are equipment vendor default settings changed (i.e. WEP keys, SSID, passwords, SNMP community strings, disabling SSID broadcasts)?
2. Is the communication encrypted using Wi-Fi Protected Access (WPA2), LEAP, VPN, SSL at 128-bit, or WEP?
3. Are encryption keys at least 128-bit and rotated at least quarterly?
4. Is wireless technology access limited to authenticated devices and users?
5. Do perimeter firewalls exist between wireless networks and the environment housing any client information at your outsourcer site?

6. Do you restrict physical access to wireless access points, wireless gateways, and wireless handheld devices?
7. Is a wireless analyzer periodically run to identify all wireless devices at your outsourcer site?

## 3. Maintaining a Vulnerability Management Program

### 3.1 Use and regularly update anti-virus software
1. Does your outsourcer have a virus scanner installed on all servers and on all workstations?
2. Is the virus scanner regularly updated?

### 3.2 Develop and maintain secure systems and applications
1. Are development, testing, and production systems updated with the latest security-related patches released by the vendors?
2. Are software and application development processes based on industry best practices and is information security included throughout the software development life cycle (SDLC) process?
3. If production data is used for testing and development purposes, is customer information sanitized before usage?
4. Are all changes to the production environment and applications formally authorized, planned, and logged before being implemented?
5. When authenticating over the Internet, are applications designed to prevent malicious users from trying to determine existing user accounts?
6. Is client information stored in cookies secured or encrypted?
7. Are controls implemented on the server side to prevent SQL injection and other bypassing of client side-input controls?

## 4. Implement Strong Access Control Measures

### 4.1 Restrict access to data by business need-to-know
1. Is access to client information restricted for outsourcer agents on a need-to-know basis?

### 4.2 Use of a unique ID for each person with computer access
1. Does your outsourcer require all users to authenticate using, at a minimum, a unique username and password?
2. If outsourcer employees, administrators, or third parties access the network remotely, is remote access software configured with unique usernames and passwords with encryption and other security features turned on?
3. Are all passwords on network devices and systems encrypted?
4. When an employee leaves the outsourcer, are the employee's user accounts and passwords immediately revoked?
5. Are all user accounts reviewed on a regular basis to ensure that malicious, out-of-date, or unknown accounts do not exist?

6. Are accounts that are not used for a lengthy amount of time (inactive accounts) automatically disabled in the system after a pre-defined period?
7. Are accounts used by vendors for remote maintenance enabled only during the time needed?
8. Are group, shared, or generic accounts and passwords prohibited?
9. Are users required to change their passwords on a predefined regular basis?
10. Is there a password policy that enforces the use of strong passwords and prevents the resubmission of previously used passwords?
11. Is there an account-lockout mechanism that blocks a malicious user from obtaining access to an account by multiple password retries or brute force?

## 4.3 Restrict physical access to client information

1. Are there multiple physical security controls, such as badges or escorts, in place that would prevent unauthorized individuals from gaining access to the facility?
2. Is equipment, such as servers, workstations, laptops, hard drives, and media containing customer information physically protected against unauthorized access?
3. Is all customer information printed on paper or received by fax protected against unauthorized access?
4. Are procedures in place to handle secure distribution and disposal of backup media and other media containing your customer information?
5. Are all media devices that store your customer information properly inventoried and securely stored?
6. Is customer information deleted or destroyed before it is physically disposed (for example, by shredding papers or degaussing backup media)?
7. Does your outsourcer encrypt data on removable media and mobile computers?

## 5. Perform Regular Monitoring and Testing of Networks and Systems

## 5.1 Track and monitor all access to networks and systems with customer information

1. Does your outsourcer log all access to systems, including root and administration, with date and time stamps?
2. Do access control logs contain successful and unsuccessful login attempts and access to audit logs?
3. Does your outsourcer have all critical system clocks and times synchronized?

4. Are the firewall, router, wireless access points, and authentication server logs regularly reviewed for unauthorized traffic?
5. Are audit logs regularly backed up, secured, and retained for at least three months online and one-year offline for all critical systems?

## 5.2 Regular testing of security systems and processes

1. Is a vulnerability scan or penetration test performed on all Internet-facing applications and systems before they go into production?
2. Is an intrusion detection or intrusion prevention system used on the network?
3. Are security alerts from an intrusion detection or intrusion prevention system (IDS/IPS) continuously monitored, and are the latest IDS/IPS signatures installed?
4. Has your outsourcer undergone a penetration or vulnerability assessment of the environment and has a professionally or nationally recognized third party performed it?

## 5.3 Maintain information security policies

1. Are information security policies, including policies for access control, application and system development, operational, network and physical security, formally documented?
2. Are information security policies and other relevant security information disseminated to all system users at your outsourcer including vendors, contractors, and business partners?
3. Are information security policies reviewed at least once a year and updated as needed?
4. Have the roles and responsibilities for information security been clearly defined within the company?
5. Is there an up-to-date information privacy and security awareness and training program in place for all system users?
6. Are employees required to sign an agreement verifying they have read and understood the security policies and procedures?
7. Is a security incident response plan formally documented and disseminated to the appropriate responsible parties?
8. Are security incidents reported to the person(s) responsible for security investigation and reviewed to determine if there are system or procedure weaknesses that require remediation?
9. Is there an incident response team ready to be deployed in case of data compromise?
10. Does your outsourcer have a policy to immediately report security breaches?

## 6. Personnel, Availability and Legal Compliance

### 6.1 Personnel risk analysis

1. Does your outsourcer screen all staff for potential security risks and require all their employees, contractors, and subcontractors to sign an appropriate confidentiality/non-disclosure agreement as well as a criminal record disclosure agreement?
2. Does your outsourcer perform a risk analysis to identify individual programmers, network analysts or other personnel upon whom the organization is excessively dependent or who are in a position to inflict significant harm?

### 6.2 Assure availability of access to customer information

1. Is all customer information stored at your outsourcer backed up regularly, stored off-site, and available for recovery?
2. Are there comprehensive, current, and tested Business Continuity and Disaster Recovery Plans in place that meet prescribed recovery times for the outsourcer functions?
3. Are customer information and systems stored at your outsourcer physically or logically separate from other process, systems, and data?

# Questions Your BPO Will Ask

Even after your have sent your RFP, received your responses, performed your due diligence, and awarded you contract, you are going to be asked a series of questions by your outsourcer. These questions are going to be from the teams that may not have been part of the proposal process and are going to reach into the depths of your company to obtain details you didn't ask and the response didn't provide. At first, this may appear to be repetitive. However, it does serve a purpose and it will be revealing to both you and your outsourcer. I provide some of the questions that may be asked as follows:

## General

1. What type of call center technology is in place today?
2. What are your call center's operating hours?
3. What happens after hours?
   a. Do calls go to voice mail?
   b. Do you offer automatic callbacks for missed calls/calls after hours?
4. How do you measure customer satisfaction?

5. Are customers tiered or segmented for either reporting or differentiated service?
   a. If so, how do you handle your tiered customers?
6. What are the goals for your call center and lines of business?
   a. For example: are you trying to improve customer satisfaction, reduce costs, or improve agent efficiency
7. Describe your different agent groups/skills and the types of calls they handle?
8. How many agents do you have to handle each skill?
9. Do you have training documentations for agents?
10. What is your daily call volume for each skill?
11. What are your service level goals?
12. What are your key performance metrics?
13. What is the length of your agent's average call?
14. Are you currently trying to manage to a targeted ASA (Average Speed of Answer)?
    a. Are you hitting the target?
15. What is the number of concurrent agents and supervisors?
16. What is the agent to supervisor ratio?
17. Do agents have shifts?
    a. Is there any overlap on the shifts?
18. What do you like about your current environment from a customer service perspective?
19. What would you like to change or improve regarding the customer's experience?
20. What is your call center's biggest challenge?
    a. What would you change in the call center if there were no budget or technology constraints?

## Applications/Customer Information

1. Are applications hosted in your data center or hosted by a third party?
   a. Describe any third party integrations being used.
2. When a contact arrives at an agent's desktop, is any information presented to the agent such as a screen pop?
3. Are applications fat applications installed on the agent desktop or thin applications accessed through a browser on the Internet?

## Desktop

1. Do you have baseline requirements for the agent desktop computer?
2. What security policies do you want to enforce on the agent desktop?
3. Is there a whitelist or blacklist of web sites to be applied for agents?

## Data Centers

1. Do you have multiple data centers?
   a. If yes, are they interconnected for redundancy/fail-over?
2. Which data centers do you want the outsourcer to connect to?

## Voice Communications

1. Will the outsourcer agents use phones connected to your PBX?
   a. If yes, will you be providing the phones or will the outsourcer?
2. Describe a typical customer call flow, such as the following
   a. Customer dials 800-000-0000 gets greeted by an IVR
   b. The IVR asks the caller to choose the type of service they need
   c. The call is transferred to the agent
3. Do you identify your customers before they are routed to an agent?
   a. Do you use separate TFNs for different lines of business?
   b. Does the caller enter their account numbers in an IVR?
4. How will calls be directed to the outsourcer call center?
   a. Will call be redirected with a TFN?
   b. Will calls be intelligently routed?
5. What are the business rules for determining contact center routing?
   a. Do you have multiple call center locations?
   b. Do they handle the same type of calls?
   c. Do you use Intelligent Call Routing?
   d. Where are your peripheral servers located?
   e. Do you currently load balance between sites?
6. Do you require calls to be transferred between agents or call centers?
   a. Are warm transfers used between different call centers?
   b. Will you need transfer and release capabilities?
7. Do you use priorities in queue?
8. Are agent callbacks required?
9. Do you service observe your agents?
   a. Is observation automated or recorded?

## Outbound

1. Describe your outbound activities.
2. Will agents work in a blended (input/outbound) environment?
3. Will the agent be dialing calls in preview mode?
4. Will campaigns be calling in predictive mode?
5. What is the average talk time for outbound calls?

## Call Recording

1. Are you recording 100% of voice/audio?
   a. How long do you retain the voice/audio recordings?
2. What percentage of screen recordings will be being recorded?
   a. How long do you retain the screen data recordings?
3. Are there any regulations that you need to follow for recordings?
4. How do you evaluate your agent recordings?
   a. Is there a formalized grading/evaluation sheet you want used?
5. Are voice analytics required?

## Data Communications

1. Will you be providing data circuits to the outsourcer for application connectivity?
   a. If not, are you looking to have data circuits dropped to your locations?
   b. If you are dropping circuits, will you be drop them to multiple outsourcer locations?
2. Are your applications using public or private IP addresses?
3. Do you know the bandwidth required to access your applications?

## Remote/Work-At-Home Agents

1. Do you have any agents currently working remotely/at home?
2. Would work at home be beneficial?

## Self Service

1. Are you considering self-help options for your customers?
   a. What options are you considering?
2. Are there repetitive activities that are offered by agents that customers could handle themselves with the right technology or solution?
3. Are there any processes that are difficult to automate?
4. Have you considered a natural language IVR for self-help?

## Reporting

1. What vital information should Supervisors see in real time?
2. What vital information should be included for reporting purposes?
3. Can you supply examples of the reports currently used?
   a. What are the intervals for each report?

# F | Change Control Activities

## Role descriptions for the change management process[29]

| Role | Description |
|---|---|
| Customer | You, as the customer, fulfill the role that requests a change due to problems encountered or new functionality require-ments; this may be at the request of the Outsourcer, but, as the customer, you own should own the request. |
| Customer Project Manager | The Customer Project Manager is the owner of the CHANGE REQUEST. |
| Outsourcer Project Manager | The Outsourcer Project Manager plans and imple-ments the change. |
| Change Control Committee | There should be two change committees that approve the change—one at your company and one at the Outsourcer. Each change committee must determine whether a CHANGE REQUEST will be implement-ed or not. |

# Activity descriptions for the change management process

| Activity | Sub-activity | Description |
|---|---|---|
| Identify potential change | Require new functionality | End-users desire new functionality and formulate a REQUIREMENT. |
| | Encounter problem | End-users encounter a problem (e.g. a bug) in the system and this leads to a PROBLEM REPORT. |
| | Request change | End-users propose a change through creation of a CHANGE REQUEST. |
| Analyze Change Request | Determine technical feasibility | NCO and DG will determine the technical feasibility of the proposed CHANGE REQUEST, leading to a CHANGE TECHNICAL FEASIBILITY. |
| | Determine costs and benefits | NCO and DG will determine the costs and benefits of the proposed CHANGE REQUEST, resulting in CHANGE COSTS AND BENEFITS. |
| Evaluate Change | | Based on the CHANGE REQUEST, its CHANGE TECHNICAL FEASIBILITY and CHANGE COSTS AND BENEFITS, NCO and DG will make a go/no-go decision. |
| Plan Change | Analyze change impact | The extent of the change (i.e. what other items the change may have to propagate in the infrastructure) is determined in a CHANGE IMPACT ANALYSIS. |
| | Create planning | A CHANGE PLANNING is created for the implementation of the change. |
| Implement change | Execute change | The change is 'programmed' and executed with the knowledge that when it propagates within the infrastructure, other parts of the infrastructure may also need to be changed. |
| | Propagate change | The changes resulting from Execute change may have to be propagated to other system parts that are influenced by it due to high dependency of the change. |

| | Test change | The change is tested to determine it works as expected and satisfies the CHANGE REQUEST. |
|---|---|---|
| | Update documentation | The DOCUMENTATION is updated to reflect the applied changes. |
| | Release change | A new SYSTEM RELEASE, which reflects the applied change, is made public. |
| Review and close change | Verify change | The implementation of the change in the new SYSTEM RELEASE is verified for the last time. |
| | Close change | This change cycle is completed, i.e. the CHANGE LOG ENTRY is wrapped. |

## Concept descriptions for the change management process

| Concept | Description |
|---|---|
| Requirement | A required functionality of a component. |
| Problem Report | Document describing a problem that cannot be solved by a level 1 help desk employee; contains items like date, contact info of person reporting the problem, what is causing the problem, location and description of the problem, action taken and disposition.[30] |
| Change Request | Document that describes the requested change and why it is important. This document can originate from PROBLEM REPORTS, system enhancements, other projects, changes in underlying systems and senior management, here summarized as REQUIREMENTS. |
| Change Log Entry | Distinct entry in the collection of all changes (e.g. for a project); consists of a CHANGE REQUEST, CHANGE TECHNICAL FEASIBILITY, CHANGE COSTS AND BENEFITS, CHANGE IMPACT ANALYSIS, CHANGE PLANNING, TEST REPORT and CHANGE VERIFICATION. |

| | |
|---|---|
| Change Technical Feasibility | Conceptually indicates whether or not "reliable" hardware, software, and technical resources are capable of meeting the needs of a proposed change (Vogl, 2004). |
| Change Costs and Benefits | The expected effort required to implement and the advantages (e.g. cost savings, increased revenue) gained by implementing the change. Also named economic feasibility (Vogl, 2004). |
| Change Impact Analysis | An assessment of how the change will impact the technology and/or business processes. For your company, you must determine if the change will impact any part of your existing operations. For your outsourcer, the analysis must determine if the change will impact their costs, business processes, or technology of your call center or any other customer's call center. |
| Change Planning | PRINCE2 defines project management as the methodology for how and when a project's objectives are to be achieved by showing the major products, milestones, activities and resources necessary to achieve the project.[31] |
| Test Report | Document that describes the procedures and results of the testing carried out for a system or component (affected by the change (IEEE, 1991). |
| Change Verification | Notification from the Outsourcer that documents whether or not the result of the change Implementation fulfills your requirements. |

# G Three Letter Acronyms (TLA)

The call center industry is full of three or more letter acronyms (TLAs) that can overwhelm even the most knowledgeable telecom engineer. This appendix is a summary TLAs used in this book, but is, by no means, representative of dictionaries such as *Newton's Telecom Dictionary*, published in over 25 editions that include explanations of approximately 25,000 teams used in the telecommunications industry.

**ABN:** Abandon Call Rate is the rate of calls disconnected after being answered divided by the calls answered.

**ACD:** Automatic Call Distributor used to route calls evenly across multiple agents. ACDs can answer inbound calls, access a database for instructions to route the call, or access data for a response, provide "hold" music or periodic messages to the caller, or just send the call to the next available agent.

**ACW:** After Call Work is the amount of time an agent spends after the call processing customer requests and completing entries into the CRM or other systems used to manage customer records.

**AHT:** Average Handle Time is the sum of time the agent is on the phone with a caller plus the time in after call work where agents complete entry into an application such as a CRM system.

**ASA:** Average Speed of Answer is the amount of time it takes an agent to answer an inbound call.

**ATM:** Automated Teller Machine, also known as an automated banking machine (ABM).

**AUR:** Agent Utilization Rate is the amount of time on the phone divided by the time they are logged in.

**CRM:** Customer Relationship Management is a well known strategy for managing a company's interaction with customer, clients, and sales. CRM systems apply the strategy for a software application used by call center agents.

**CSAT:** Customer Satisfaction is the measure of the overall satisfaction of the interaction between agent and customer.

**CSO:** Chief Security Officer is typically a corporate officer that stipulates the security methods and procedures to be used by their company.

**DNIS:** Dialed Number Identification Service, which provides the number dialed when calling an 800 or 900 number. DNIS may be used in simple call routing where the DNIS of a TFN is used to route the call to an associated agent skill.

**DR:** Disaster Recovery

**DMZ:** DeMilitarized Zone that describes a physical or logical network between a secure internal network to an untrusted network such as the Internet. DMZ is used as an additional layer or security and is sometimes referred to as a perimeter network.

**FCR:** First Call Resolution is where an agent resolves the issues of the customer in a single (i.e. the first) call.

**HIPPA:** Health Insurance Portability and Accountability Act enacted in 1996 by the U.S. Congress.

**IaaS:** Infrastructure as a Service, in this context, hosts telephony components such as an IVR, dialer, voice recorder, ACD, etc.

**ICR:** Intelligent Call Routing is a computer application that is usually an adjunct to an ACD to route calls to a specific agent, skill, or location based on programming of business rules.

**ITIL:** Information Technology Infrastructure Library originated in the 1980s by the British government to improve the quality and reduce the costs of IT services.

**IVR:** Interactive Voice Response is a system that verbal provides callers with numeric options to navigate its menu of options. Numeric digits may be spoken through a telephone handset or entered from a telephone keypad. IVRs may collect digits such as account numbers and "speak" responses from a database lookup. (Also referred to as a VRU (Voice Response Unit).

**LAN:** Local Area Network is a short distance network typically bounded by the walls of a building.

**LEC:** Local Exchange Carrier—the carrier for the last mile of long distance voice carrier or a WAN. Typically, the LEC is the local carrier for the geographic region where a circuit is terminated.

**NAT:** Network Address Translation is an Internet standard used to translate an IP address from an internal network to an IP address in an open or external network such as the Internet.

**MSA:** Master Services Agreement is a contract that outlines the responsibilities and obligations of one party with another where multiple agreements are in place.

**PaaS:** Platform as a Service offers the ability to develop applications entirely on the Internet without the cost of purchasing and managing the underlying hardware and software in a hosted environment.

**PBX:** Private Branch eXchange is a small version of a telephone company central office. PBXs can handle both inbound and outbound calls, but are more flexible and can be programmed to meet your business requirements.

**PDA:** Personal Digital Assistant, originally coined by Steve Jobs in 1992 to describe the Apple Newton. It is used as a generic term to describe devices from a smart phone to tablet.

**PSTN:** Public Switched Telephone Network that has traditionally carried voice and fax communications. More recently, the PSTN carried data using modems up to 56 kilobytes.

**PSTN/IN:** PSTN Intelligent Network

**QA:** Quality Assurance is the process used to monitor calls for agent compliance with service objectives.

**RFI:** Request for Information

**RFP:** Request for Proposal

**SaaS**: Software as a Service where a hosed company provides applications over the Internet.

**SIP:** Session Internet Protocol is a popular Voice over IP (VoIP) standard that enables two or more people to make phone calls to each other using the Internet to carry the call.

**SLA:** Service Level Agreement, in this context, is a contact establishing the performance metrics between a company and an outsourcer. For example, a service level might stipulate the maximum and average number of seconds for inbound call to be answered.

**SMS:** Short Message Service used for text communications on mobile phones operating on cellular carrier systems

**TFN:** Toll Free Number is a telephone number, usually available for long-distance, where the called party (your company or your outsourcer) is billed instead of the caller (agent).

**UC:** Unified Communications is the integration of real-time communications between agent and your outsourcer using a consistent user interface and user experience at the agent desktop.

**VoIP:** Voice over Internet Protocol is a protocol used to delivery voice and multimedia over the Internet rather than through the public switched telephone network (PSTN).

**WAN:** Wide Area Network supporting VoIP and data in a geographic area that is typically bigger than a city or metropolitan.

**WOMMA:** Word of Mouth Marketing Association, WOMMA (http://womma.org) that offers training, best practices, standards, and best practices to its members.

**WFM:** Work Force Management is software that is used to manage workload and staffing requirements across multiple skills, lines of business, and call center sites.

# H End Notes

## Introduction

1. July 2007,
   http://www.dailygalaxy.com/my_weblog/
   2007/07/42-hitchikers-g.html
2. Julie Wolf, "The 1982 Recession,"
   http://www.pbs.org/wgbh/amex/re-
   agan/peopleevents/pande06.html

## Rule 1: Rules Are Meant to Be Broken

3. Sculley, J. and Byme, J. Odyssey : *Pepsi to
   Apple : A Journey of Adventure, Ideas, and
   the Future*, (New York: Harper & Row,
   1987), p.157

## Rule 2: Ask "Why Outsource?"

4. September 2010, http://www.nashuatele-
   graph.com/news/840346-196/dai-
   ly-twip---emma-nutt-becomes-the.html
5. March 2009,
   http://pbskids.org/wayback/tech1900/
   phone.html
6. *BPO: Higher Quality, Competitive Costs*,
   Brendan Read, October 12, 2009,
   http://www.newsfactor.com/story.xht-
   ml?story_id=69067

## Rule 3: Define an Outsourcing Approach

7. Dan Blacharski, "The Basics of Business Process Outsourcing," *Sourcingmag.com*, April 5, 2006, http://www.sourcingmag.com/content/c060405a.asp

## Rule 5: Communication Is the Key to Customer Relationship

8. *Dell's Customer Contact Center Operations in India*, ICMR Case Studies and Management Resources, March 2009, http://www.icmrindia.org/casestudies/catalogue/Marketing/MKTG152.htm

## Rule 8: Integrate Social Networking

9. "An Introduction to WOM Marketing", December, 2009, http://womma.org/wom101/
10. Robin Wauters, "Zuckerberg Admits Facebook Now Has 200 Million Users," TechCrunch.com., April 2009, http://www.techcrunch.com/2009/04/08/zuckerberg-welcomes-200-millionth-facebook-user-wants-to-know-how-it-affected-your-life/
11. June, 2011, http://www.facebook.com/press/info.php?statistics
12. J. Swartz, Social media like Twitter change customer service, *USA Today*, 2009, http://www.usatoday.com/tech/news/2009-11-18-twitterserve18_ST_N.htm?csp=Tech
13. J. Swartz, 2009

## Rule 9: Evaluate Self-Help Customer Service

14. IBM Simon, December, 2009, http://en.wikipedia.org/wiki/IBM_Simon.

## Rule 13: Evaluate Voice Communication Options

15. Zeus Kerravala, "What are SIP trunks (and why your need one)?," SearchVoIP, Oct 2008, http://searchvoip.techtarget.com.au/articles/27253-What-are-SIP-trunks-and-why-you-need-one-

## Rule 15: Manage the Potential Impact of Risks

16. C Tremper, "How to Develop a Risk Management Plan," http://www.wikihow.com/Develop-a-Risk-Management-Plan
17. Risk Management, Jan 2011, http://en.wikipedia.org/wiki/Risk_management

## Rule 25: Establish Security Guidelines

18. Information Security Guidelines,
http://the-dma.org/guidelines/informationsecurity.shtml
19. L.B. Baker and J. Finkel, "Sony PlayStation suffers massive data breach," *Reuters*, April 26, 2011,
http://www.reuters.com/article/2011/04/26/us-sony-stolden-data-idUSTRE73P6WB20110426

## Rule 27: Define Desktop Security for the Agents

20. Microsoft TechNet, "Introduction (Implementing Common Desktop Management Scenarios with the Group Policy Management Console)," March 2005.

## Rule 37: Monitor Customer Satisfaction in All Media

21. R. Reynolds, "a new look at THE TOP 20 Contact Center Metrics," Nov 2006, http://multichannelmerchant.com/opsandfulfillment/contact_center_metrics_112006/
22. M. Brandau, M, "Speed matters when it comes to Facebook," May 2011,
http://nrn.com/article/speed-matters-when-it-comes-facebook
23. K. Carter, "Analysis of email and phone queuing systems in a world wide contact network," May 2008, Submitted to the MIT Sloan School of Management and the Department of Aeronautics and Astronautics, http://dspace.mit.edu/bitstream/handle/1721.1/43832/262695753.pdf?sequence=1

## Rule 38: Monitor Call Quality

24. "30 tips to improve your call quality monitoring," Jan 2001, http://www.callcentrehelper.com/tips-to-improve-your-call-quality-monitoring-4732.htm

## Rule 39: Communicate When Technology Breaks

25. S. Davis, 1999, "Making Your Command Center a Success" http://www.davislogic.com/articles.htm

## Rule 40: Things Change

26. ITIL, 2011, http://www.itil-officialsite.com

## Rule 41: Disasters Happen

27. "WHO maintains 2 billion estimate for likely H1N1 cases," *Reuters*, Tue Aug 4, 2009 12:38pm EDT, http://www.reuters.com/article/healthNews/idUSTRE57 34VG20090804

## Appendix D: Assessing Security

28. Excerpted and reprinted with permission from NCO Information Security Standards, Paul Lagacey, NCO

## Appendix F: Change Control Activities

29. Change management (engineering), Jan 2011 http://en.wikipedia.org/wiki/Change_management_(engi-neering)
30. A. Dennis, B.H. Wixom, and.D. Tegarden, *System Analysis & Design: An Object-Oriented Approach with UML*, Hoboken, New York (New York: John Wiley & Sons, Inc., 2002)
31. *What Is Prince2*, (Jan 2011) http://www.prince2.com/what-is-prince2.asp

## About the Author

Geoffrey A. Best started in the computer industry in the 1970's and has worked with call centers for over 20 years. His career has taken him from computer aided mapping and 911 emergency dispatch systems, to computer telephony applications and today's call center systems. Geoffrey has worked and consulted around the world with utilities, communications, manufacturing, banking, and insurance companies. His experience has provided him with insight into the systems and methods that companies use to operate their call centers and service their customers. This experience has given Geoffrey a unique perspective of how customer expectations have changed over the past decades and how call center solutions have evolved to satisfy them.

# 42 Rules Program

A lot of people would like to write a book, but only a few actually do. Finding a publisher, and distributing and marketing the book are challenges that prevent even the most ambitious authors from getting started.

If you want to be a successful author, we'll provide you the tools to help make it happen. Start today by completing a book proposal at our website http://42rules.com/write/.

For more information, email info@superstarpress.com or call 408-257-3000.

## Other Happy About Books

### 42 Rules of Employee Engagement

Susan Stamm will inspire and challenge you to create a unique workspace with your team that attracts and inspires high performance, commitment and authentic work relationships.

Paperback: $19.95
eBook: $14.95

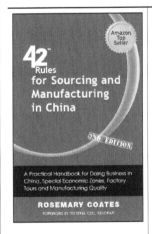

### 42 Rules for Sourcing and Manufacturing in China

Through over 20 extraordinary executive interviews, Rosemary Coates captured the essence of sourcing and manufacturing in China.

Paperback: $19.95
eBook: $14.95

### *Happy About Customer Service?*

Do you want to develop your customer service standards so that you consistently, and to the endless pleasure of your customers, deliver customer service excellence? If, your answer to this is YES, MOST DEFINITELY YES, then read this book.

Paperback: $19.95
eBook: $14.95

### *Offshoring Secrets*

In this book, Utkarsh has drawn upon his years of experience and interactions with various people in the industry in setting up and running a successful India operation.

Paperback: $19.95
eBook: $14.95

Purchase these books at Happy About
http://happyabout.com/
or at other online and physical bookstores.

## A Message From Super Star Press™

Thank you for your purchase of this 42 Rules Series book. It is available online at:
http://www.happyabout.com/42rules/outsourcingcallcenter.php
or at other online and physical bookstores. To learn more about contributing to books in the 42 Rules series, check out
http://superstarpress.com.

Please contact us for quantity discounts at
sales@superstarpress.com.

If you want to be informed by email of upcoming books, please email
bookupdate@superstarpress.com.

Made in the USA
Lexington, KY
26 September 2013